THE OUTER CITY: GEOGRAPHICAL CONSEQUENCES OF THE URBANIZATION OF THE SUBURBS

Peter O. Muller
Temple University

RESOURCE PAPER NO. 75-2

Copyright 1976
by the
Association of American Geographers
1710 Sixteenth Street, N.W.
Washington, D.C. 20009

Library of Congress Card Number 76-029264
ISBN 0-89291-114-x
Supported by the AAG and by a grant from
the National Science Foundation

FOREWORD

In 1968, the Commission on College Geography of the Association of American Geographers published its first Resource Paper,*Theories of Urban Location*, by Brian J. L. Berry. In 1974, coinciding with the termination of NSF funding for the Commission, Resource Paper number 28 appeared, *The Underdevelopment and Modernization of the Third World*, by Anthony R. deSouza and Philip W. Porter. Of the many CCG activities, the Resource Papers Series became an effective means for permitting both teachers and students to keep abreast of developments in the field.

Because of the popularity and usefulness of the Resource Papers, the AAG applied for and received a modest grant from NSF to continue to produce Resource Papers and to put the series on a self-supporting basis. The present Resource Papers Panel subscribes to the original purposes of the Series, which are quoted below:

> The Resource Papers have been developed as expository documents for the use of both the student and the instructor. They are experimental in that they are designed to supplement existing texts and to fill a gap between significant research in American geography and readily accessible materials. The papers are concerned with important concepts or topics in modern geography and focus on one of three general themes: geographic theory; policy implications; or contemporary social relevance. They are designed to implement a variety of undergraduate college geography courses at the introductory and advanced level.

In an effort to increase the utility of these papers, the Panel has attempted to be particularly sensitive to the currency of materials for undergraduate geography courses and to the writing style of these papers.

The Resource Papers are developed, printed, and distributed under the auspices of the Association of American Geographers, with partial funding from a National Science Foundation grant. The ideas presented in these papers do not imply endorsement by the AAG.

Many individuals have assisted in producing these Resource Papers, and we wish to acknowledge those who assisted the Panel in reviewing the authors' prospectuses, in reading and commenting on the various drafts, and in making helpful suggestions. The Panel also acknowledges the perceptive suggestions and editorial assistance of Jane F. Castner of the AAG Central Office.

Salvatore J. Natoli
Educational Affairs Director
Association of American Geographers
Project Director and Editor, Resource Papers Series

Resource Papers Panel:

John F. Lounsbury, Arizona State University
Mark S. Monmonier, Syracuse University
Harold A. Winters, Michigan State University

PREFACE

This Resource Paper was conceived and written expressly for the beginning geography or urban studies college student, to introduce him to the evolution and contemporary functioning of America's suburbs. Since this vitally important topic is not covered in depth in urban studies textbooks, and is all but totally neglected in urban geography texts, this Resource Paper can be used most effectively as a textbook supplement in either introductory or intermediate urban courses. Instructors using a different approach can employ this Paper as the basis for a modular unit in a wide variety of introductory, advanced, and regional North America human geography courses. This material has met with equal success when taught in undergraduate urban geography courses and in interdisciplinary urban studies courses composed of history, sociology, political science, American studies, urban economics, planning, and general social science majors.

This material has been used most effectively as an entire course with suburban students at Temple's Ambler Campus outside Philadelphia. A great deal of stimulating classroom discussion was generated, and recently the instructor has been hard-pressed to cover the contents of this Resource Paper within a 15-week semester.

Local illustrations should be emphasized whenever possible. The twenty metropolitan "vignettes" of the AAG's Comparative Metropolitan Analysis Project (published by Ballinger in 1976, with eleven in individual paperback form) are valuable in this regard. Residents of metropolitan areas not covered in the vignettes can easily make use of local newspapers and magazines. Periodicals which frequently cover suburban topics are *The New York Times, Washington Post, U.S. News and World Report, Business Week, Fortune, Society, Public Interest,* and the whole range of scholarly journals in urban-related disciplines. Instructors and students alike are encouraged to make use of the Bibliography included in this Resource Paper. It is designed to be of use as a basic research tool, and its currency should extend its utility into at least the early 1980s.

Finally, readers should be aware that only a broad national coverage has been attempted here, and local variations can be expected to occur. Nevertheless, the basic social and economic trends discussed herein operate in every North American metropolis, and the author counts himself among those urbanists who insist that much more scholarly attention must be focused on suburbia if we are to comprehend the forces which are shaping our nation's current and future urbanization.

Peter O. Muller
Temple University

CONTENTS

PREFACE v
I. THE OUTER CITY IN SPACE AND TIME 1
    Introduction 1
    The Historical Evolution of Suburban America 3
    Intraurban Transportation and the Stages of Suburban Growth 5
    Afterword 8
II. THE ORGANIZATION OF SUBURBAN SOCIAL SPACE AND ITS HUMAN CONSEQUENCES 11
    Suburban Residential Patterns and Their Interpretation 11
    Contemporary Urbanization Influences 13
    Community Form, the Emerging Mosaic Culture, and Suburban Lifestyles 13
    The Intensifying Heterogeneity of Suburban Society 17
    The Segregation of Suburban Social Groups 18
    Black Suburban Settlement Types 19
    Mechanisms Perpetuating Suburban Racial Segregation 20
    The Suburban Dual Housing Market and Its Impact 20
    Exclusionary Zoning and the Persistence of Closed Suburbs 23
    The Continuing Legal Struggle Against Suburban Exclusion 24
    The Failure of Housing Programs to Open the Suburbs 26
    Human Consequences of Suburban Exclusionism 26
III. THE NEW ROLE OF THE SUBURBS IN METROPOLITAN ECONOMIC GEOGRAPHY 29
    The Decentralization of Retailing 29
    The Superregional Mall of the 1970s 31
    The Intrametropolitan Deconcentration of Employment 32
    The Suburbanization of Manufacturing Since 1960 33
    Industrial Parks in the Outer City 34
    Current Trends in the Location of Suburban Office Activity 35
    Minicities and Suburban Spatial Organization 40
    Minicities, Beltways, and the Emerging Spatial Structure of
      the Outer City 42
    Suburban Avoidance of the Central City and the Metropolitan Future 44
BIBLIOGRAPHY 47

LIST OF FIGURES

1. Chicago Suburb x
2. The Changing Spatial Form of the Twentieth-Century American Metropolis 2
3. Percentage Share of Total U.S. Population Change, 1900-1970 3
4. Intraurban Transport Eras and Metropolitan Growth Patterns 5
5. Intrametropolitan Density Gradients, 1910-1963 7
6. The Expansion of Metropolitan Chicago 8
7. 1970 Per Capita Income by Minor Civil Divisions, Philadelphia SMSA 12
8. Black Suburbanization Trends, 1900-1970 18
9. Spatial Forms of Black Suburbanization 19
10. Internal Economic Geography of the Suburban Minicity: King of Prussia, Pennsylvania 41
11. Forecasted 1980 Travel Desires Among Internal Districts of Metropolitan Baltimore 43

LIST OF TABLES

1. Relative Percentages of Urban Population Growth, 1900-1970 4
2. Suburban Percentage of Total SMSA Population for the Fifteen Largest 1970 SMSAs, 1900-1970   4
3. Selected Data on the Deconcentration of Intrametropolitan Economic Activity 30

CHICAGO SUBURB

by Carl Sandbag

Hog Barbecuer for the World,
School Segregator, Mower of Lawns,
Player with Golf Clubs and the Nation's Wife Swapper;
Bigoted, snobbish, flaunting,
Suburb of the White Collars.
They tell me you are lazy, and I believe them; for I have seen your
  women in the super-market parking lots, tipping box boys to load
  their station wagons.
And they tell me you are brutal, and my reply is: At the stations of
  your commuter trains, I have seen old ladies trampled by men in
  quest of seats on the shady side.
And they tell me your soil is rotten and vengeful, and I answer: Yes,
  it is true, for I have seen crab grass killed and rise up to grow
  again.
But still, I turn to those who sneer at this, my suburb, and I give
  them back the sneer and say to them:
Come and show me another town with eight drive-in mortuaries and a
  Colonel Sanders on every block;
Show me a suburb with mortgage payments so high that men worry
  themselves into heart attacks at forty,
    Debt-ridden,
    Overdrawn,
    Embezzling,
    Financing, defaulting, re-financing,
But pleased as punch to be Hog Barbecuers for the World, School
  Segregators, Mowers of Lawns, Players with Golf Clubs and
  Champion Wife Swappers of the Nation.

I. THE OUTER CITY IN SPACE AND TIME

Suburbia is becoming the city of the '70s.   L. Masotti

A critical new balance in the organization of the American metropolis has been struck.
   B. Schwartz

Introduction

Though enlivened by *MAD*'s sense of satiric humor, "Chicago Suburb" (Figure 1) depicts a false image of suburbia which is still accepted by far too many Americans. This perception derives from the anti-suburban bias that marked the writing of many journalists, novelists, and social critics in the 1950s and 60s. Repeated vilification has produced a distorted popular stereotype now known as the "suburban myth" (see Berger, 1971; Donaldson, 1969). Until recently, a similar view was also shared and accepted unquestioningly by social scientists. It is only in the last few years that a critical mass of urban researchers has been able to assemble an accurate picture of current suburban patterns, one which, though still incomplete, begins to shed some light on the ways in which contemporary suburbanization processes—spatial and otherwise—are unfolding.

Myths, once ingrained, are not easily dispelled. However, the much-maligned American suburb must be reassessed, because the image of a homogeneous middle class population of core city commuters living in split-level "little boxes" with cracked picture windows, surrounded by lawns full of crab grass and pursuing a standardized, superficial, and highly conformist lifestyle, even if once true in some respects, is wholly inconsistent with the diversity and dynamics of the contemporary suburban scene. Stated simply, suburbia in the 1970s constitutes "a whole new urban ball game" (Masotti, 1973). The recent emergence of suburban America requires a reexamination. This Resource Paper deals with the characteristics and challenges of contemporary suburbanization and seeks in particular to elucidate the evolution of its general spatial structures, i.e., its human geography.

Urbanization trends in the United States today indicate suburbia to be the essence of the contemporary American city. It is now patently evident that the suburbs are no longer "sub" to the "urb" in the traditional sense. Chiefly as a result of the recent intrametropolitan deconcentration[1] of economic activity following in the wake of the enormous population exodus from the central cities in the last quarter century, suburbia in the late 1970s is emerging as *the outer city*. Expressed geographically, this transformation involves a shift from the tightly focused single-core urban region of the past to the widely dispersed multi-nodal metropolis of today (Figure 2). As a result, large new outlying urban centers of considerable locational pull have rapidly emerged in the seventies, and such suburban minicities as Newport Center (Los Angeles), Schaumburg (Chicago), Cherry Hill (Philadelphia), and the Galleria (Houston) are already widely known. The significance of this metamorphosis is that conventional center-periphery models of metropolitan spatial structure are no longer inclusive enough for understanding contemporary urban geography. The processes which recently culminated in the spatial reorganization of the metropolis began to operate noticeably in the early post World War Two period and have greatly accelerated since the late 1950s; but many of these forces are rooted in earlier suburbanization trends in the half century preceding the War, and particularly in the two decades following the widespread introduction of the automobile around 1920.

The 1970 census clearly documents the vast scale and new dominance of America's suburbs. Although these data are already several years old (and are rendered modest by newer interim census reports), the suburban trends they indicate persist into the 1970s,[2] and they still paint a vivid portrait of a decidedly suburban nation:

- 37.6 percent (76.3 million) of the U.S. population resided in the suburbs in 1970, with 31.4 percent (63.8 million) living in central cities and 31.0 percent (63.0 million) in rural areas; the latest 1975 population estimates show these proportions to be 39.1 percent suburban, 29.6 percent central city, and 31.3 percent rural

---

[1] Deconcentration refers to the *general* increase of people or activity in the suburbs with respect to the central city; decentralization refers to the *specific* relocation of people and activities from city to suburb.

[2] Census Bureau estimates show an 8.4 percent increase in the nation's suburban population between 1970 and 1975.

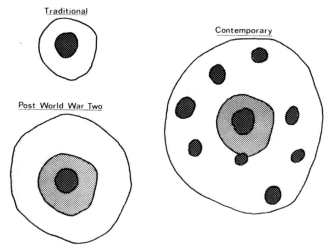

Figure 2. The Changing Spatial Form of the Twentieth-Century American Metropolis.

- 54.2 percent of the nation's 1970 metropolitan population lived outside central cities; in the 25 largest metropolitan areas 62.7 percent resided in the suburban ring
- in the 1960s suburbs grew more than five times faster than the central cities, capturing 84 percent of all urban population growth and more than 70 percent of the total national increase
- by 1970 the suburbs for the first time recorded more housing units (24 million) than either the central cities which spawned them (22.6 million) or nonmetropolitan areas (22.4 million)
- in the 1960s the suburban share of metropolitan employment in the largest metropolitan areas grew by 44 percent compared to a seven percent decrease for the central cities; latest available data show a total suburban job increase of more than three million in the 1965-1974 period, and that by the end of 1973 suburban employment nationwide exceeded the cities' job total for the first time
- suburban political power has expanded to the point where it now accounts for the largest bloc of seats in the U.S. House of Representatives (131 suburban; 130 rural; 102 central city; and 72 mixed districts with many partially suburban) as well as control of several key state legislatures

One must temper the interpretation of these data by the continuing difficulty of defining exactly what constitutes a suburb (for a current attempt see Lineberry, 1975). The Urbanized Area, as defined by the census, includes what is today only a portion of the urban fringe; in any case, the rapid expansion of the outer suburbs in the last few years almost certainly has rendered most 1970 Urbanized Areas obsolete. A large number of researchers utilize the "outside central cities" portions of the nation's 243 SMSAs (Standard Metropolitan Statistical Areas). Some have criticized this use of outer ring counties on the grounds that such areas may include nonmetropolitan population, but the recent work of geographers with the Daily Urban System notion has shown that, if anything, SMSAs tend to undercount the outlying urban population. Consequently, the outer ring definition of the census will be our "data base" as well, unless otherwise indicated. Even with these definitions, several million suburban residents of metropolitan areas containing central cities of less than 50,000 remain unaccounted for. Also excluded are *de facto* suburbanites by lifestyle and spatial behavior who live within the political limits of central cities either by recent annexation of former suburban territory or retarded development of once remote fringe areas such as New York's Staten Island Borough of Richmond (300,000 in 1970) or Philadelphia's Northeast (ca. 500,000). From these observations any number of upwardly revised calculations of the total U.S. suburban population can be offered, and even estimates in the 100 million range should probably not be considered excessive. When not working with comparative statistical measures of suburbanization, Anthony Downs' operational definition of suburbia best reflects the reality encountered by active workers in the field:

> ... *suburbs* refers to all parts of all metropolitan areas outside of central cities. It therefore includes unincorporated areas as well as [18,000] suburban municipalities. Communities that are considered *suburbs* by this definition range in population from a few hundred to over 80,000, in land-use composition from entirely residential to almost entirely industrial with nearly all possible mixtures in between, and in distance from the central city from immediate adjacency to over a hundred miles away. (1973, pp. viii, 201)

However one regards the data, it all adds up to the ongoing *urbanization of the suburbs*. Old distinctions between city and suburb are disappearing. In fact, America's largest "city" in 1970 was suburban New York (8.9 million). In partial recognition of that status, the federal government designated Greater New York's Long Island salient (Nassau and Suffolk Counties) the nation's first all-suburban SMSA in 1972:

> If [these counties] were a city, they would be the fourth largest city in the nation.... While these two counties have close economic and social ties to the City of New York, they also have an independent economic and social base which is larger than that of all but a handful of the nation's largest metropolitan areas. (*Newsday*, 1973, pp. 28-29)

1970 census data further point up the urbanization of suburbia by showing greater scale and heterogeneity in the most recent wave of suburban migration. As the quality of city life erodes, those able to move to a more desirable or to a newer residential environment have increasingly done so. Latent desires to follow are undoubtedly widespread among the less advantaged residual central city population, but the existence of social and economic barriers, especially involving access to available housing, prevents this. Nevertheless, a more socioeconomically diverse population has entered suburbia since 1960, and one sees increasing signs of urbanization in today's suburbs in the form of ethnic neighborhoods, apartment complexes, entertainment facilities, and a rise in the number of small households comprised of couples whose children have grown up and left home.

Much of this latest intrametropolitan population dispersal can also be attributed to the suburbanization of economic activity, especially employment opportunities. The deconcentration of these activities appears to be one of the strongest forces in sustaining the current urbanization of the suburbs, and is reflected in a growing sense of true economic independence from the central city. Contemporary suburbia offers an attractive locational alternative for most metropolitan activities and now shares, and even usurps, nearly all the exclusively downtown-bound functions of the past. A few of these functions which are currently decentralizing successfully are international corporation headquarters, financial institutions with extensive regional operations, major league sports, and musical and theatrical events of national importance. To be sure, urbanization has also had its negative side-effects in suburbia as the outer city now shares many of the central city's social, political, environmental, and transportation problems.

As the suburbs approach self-sufficiency increasing numbers of its residents avoid the central city altogether. Understandably, this trend is having a devastating impact on big cities because those catalytic activities and talented leaders needed to reverse the present exodus are themselves pulling up stakes for destinations beyond the city line.

The human geographical consequences of the urbanization of the suburbs are multi-faceted and far-reaching. Clearly, there is a need for geographers to conduct more research on contemporary suburbia, particularly on regional variations in suburbanization processes and patterns. But in this compact survey only the major dimensions of suburban social and economic spatial organization can be identified; however a general understanding of these geographical relationships can provide a useful basis for considering the problems and challenges now facing the outer city. Accordingly, following a very brief overview of the historical evolution of American suburbs in the remainder of this chapter, Chapter II will treat the organization of suburban social space and its human consequences and Chapter III the new role of the suburbs in metropolitan economic geography.

The Historical Evolution of Suburban America[3]

Although the nation's suburbs have but recently emerged as a dominant metropolitan force, they are not a distinctively new type of urban settlement. De-

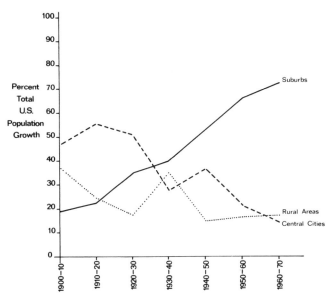

Figure 3. Percentage Share of Total U.S. Population Change, 1900-1970. Source: U.S. Census of Population: 1960. Selected Area Reports: SMSAs, Social and Economic Data for Persons in SMSAs by Residence Inside or Outside Central City, Final Report PC (3)-1D (1960-70 updated figures were computed from the 1970 census by the author).

velopment of the city fringe extends back to the dawn of urbanization, and the modern American process of suburbanization—the sustained growth of city edges at a rate faster than that of central areas—has been in evidence for the last century and a quarter (Jackson, 1973). Census data on suburbanization are available from 1900 onward, and these twentieth-century growth trends are displayed by decade for the national, metropolitan, and selected individual levels of generalization in Figure 3 and Tables 1 and 2.

The American Rural Ethic and Suburban Evolution

Central to an understanding of suburban evolution is a set of values and beliefs deeply ingrained in American native culture: the so-called rural ideal (see Zelinsky, 1973, esp. pp 41-64; Tuan, 1974, pp. 236-238). The roots of this ideal stem from the tenets of Jeffersonian democracy with its emphasis on the healthful farming life in the small agrarian community of equal participation and control over local government. Inherent in this rural ethic is a powerful popular image against living in cities, which are viewed as symbols of corruption with their class divisions, social inequities, and disorder. Thus, al-

---

[3] Space limits the publication of all but a capsule summary of the chapter-length statement on the historical geography of suburbia originally prepared for this Resource Paper. Interested readers may obtain a manuscript copy of this evolutionary survey by writing to the author.

TABLE 1. RELATIVE PERCENTAGES OF URBAN POPULATION GROWTH, 1900–1970

Decade	Population Growth Rate Of Cities	Population Growth Rate Of Suburbs	Percent Total SMSA Growth In Cities	Percent Total SMSA Growth In Suburbs	Suburban Growth Per 100 Increase In Central City
1900–10	37.1	23.6	72.1	27.9	38.7
1910–20	27.7	20.0	71.6	28.4	39.6
1920–30	24.3	32.3	59.3	40.7	68.5
1930–40	5.6	14.6	41.0	59.0	144.0
1940–50	14.7	35.9	40.7	59.3	145.9
1950–60	10.7	48.5	23.8	76.2	320.3
1960–70	5.3	28.2	4.4	95.6	2153.1

Source: Same as Figure 3.

though it came to be respected as an efficient producer, exciting activity center, and pacesetter, the city itself was otherwise perceived as inhumane, and for the past century and a half most Americans have lived in "one of the world's most urbanized countries as if it were a wilderness in both time and space" (Warner, 1972, p. 4). Others are even more blunt in their assessment, concluding that the city has been callously regarded from a purely utilitarian perspective as a "service station" for absorbing and integrating both domestic and foreign immigrants into the mainstream of American life (Kristol, 1972; Elazar, 1972). One can therefore judge the success of the city by how effectively and rapidly it acculturates newcomers so that they can depart for the suburbs, increasingly the preserve of American nativist culture in face of the growing ethnic pluralism of city society (Vance, 1972, p. 186).

Historians have traced American suburbs from earliest colonial times. Fringe settlements around such cities as New Orleans, Boston, and Philadelphia performed vital manufacturing, warehousing and other commercial functions in the preindustrial period, and proved to be of great importance later when the central town expanded, by incorporating the outer centers and their activities, to form the complete city. Early suburbs also housed the poor as well as brothels and other illicit activities. Their negative image developed as social outcasts, sin spots, and obnoxious industries concentrated there but, as the colonial city grew larger, late preindustrial suburbs also assumed a more positive role as a "refuge" for the wealthy from the growing disorder of urban life. The latter perception intensified when large-scale urbanization became an unavoidable by-product of national economic growth in the early nineteenth

TABLE 2. SUBURBAN PERCENTAGE OF TOTAL SMSA POPULATION FOR THE FIFTEEN LARGEST 1970 SMSAs, 1900–1970

Metropolis	1900	1910	1920	1930	1940	1950	1960	1970
New York+	*32.2	32.4	33.8	36.2	36.1	38.9	47.3	51.2
Los Angeles	44.9	*37.4	*36.6	*40.7	42.8	46.5	53.2	54.9
Chicago	18.5	*19.1	20.4	*24.1	25.7	30.1	42.9	51.8
Philadelphia	31.6	31.7	32.8	37.8	39.6	43.6	53.9	59.6
Detroit	*33.1	24.1	*23.9	*28.0	31.7	38.7	55.6	64.0
San Francisco	24.5	26.7	28.4	31.9	35.9	45.7	58.2	65.4
Washington	26.4	25.7	23.5	27.6	31.5	46.8	63.2	73.6
Boston	57.5	58.1	*60.0	64.0	65.1	66.8	73.1	76.7
Pittsburgh	*58.3	63.7	*66.6	66.9	67.7	69.4	74.9	78.3
St. Louis	30.4	33.4	33.7	40.7	44.3	51.2	64.4	73.7
Baltimore	26.2	27.5	*18.7	*22.4	24.6	34.8	47.9	56.3
Cleveland	17.2	*15.1	*18.0	*27.6	*30.7	40.3	54.1	63.6
Houston	*30.0	*31.9	*25.9	*18.6	*27.3	*36.3	*33.9	*38.0
Minneapolis-St. Paul	20.4	16.9	*15.5	16.6	19.4	27.6	46.3	59.0
Dallas	*79.8	*65.8	*54.7	*43.2	*44.1		*39.3	*45.7
Mean	35.4	34.0	32.8	35.1	37.8	44.1	53.9	60.8
Mean for all SMSAs	37.9	35.4	34.0	35.4	37.3	41.4	48.6	54.2

+ Standard Consolidated Area data.
* First census following greater than ten percent territorial annexation by the central city.
Sources: Same as Figure 3; Jackson, 1972, pp. 443, 445.

century. The onset of industrialization launched the "romantic" suburb movement after 1830 in which the rural ideal was directly superimposed on city life for the affluent (Thorns, 1972, p. 65). Peri-urban countryside was now viewed as the perfect place for residential location; city-country compatibility would be enhanced by combining the well-paying city job with the very real advantages of living in a semi-rural suburban home. Indeed, such new communities were so successful that by mid-century the renowned landscape architect Frederick Law Olmsted was moved to predict that "no great town can long exist without great suburbs" (Jackson, 1973, p. 204).

Intraurban Transportation and the Stages of Suburban Growth

Modern suburbanization began early in the second half of the nineteenth century as urban residents increasingly were able to live on the fringes of the city. More specifically, this trend was initiated and then perpetuated through the combination of pre-1850 peripheral settlement with more efficient means of urban transport and the beginnings of residential segregation in the large city (Singleton, 1973, p. 45). Since transportation technology has been a significant force in shaping suburban spatial structure for the last century (see Tarr, 1973; Holt, 1972; Schaeffer and Sclar, 1975, pp. 8-60), it is profitable to trace the growth of modern suburbs within a framework of urban transport eras. The following four-stage scheme is based upon key innovations affecting movement and spatial organization within the metropolis: the Walking-Horsecar Era (pre-1850-late 1880s); the Electric Streetcar Era (late 1880s-1920); the Recreational Automobile Era (1920-1945); and the postwar Freeway Era (Adams, 1970). Within this scheme two general forms of urban growth can be observed: uniform transport surface conditions (Eras 1 and 3) allowing directional freedom of movement and a circular development pattern, and movement network biases (Eras 2 and 4) producing an irregularly shaped metropolis in which axial growth along radial arterials outruns that of the less accessible interstices. Figure 4 shows the cumulative impact of the four transport eras on the overall geographical pattern of urban spread. In turn, each era made several distinctive contributions to suburban development.

Walking-Horsecar Era

Prior to the 1850s, the American city was a small, tightly compact urban settlement (Figure 4, Era 1) in which walking was the dominant mode of movement. With people and activities concentrated within walking distance, land uses and social groups intermingled almost at random. Only prosperous merchants and the wealthy maintained their social distance, and the coming of the railroad after the mid-1830s permitted them to live entirely outside

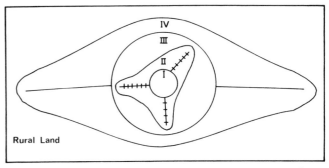

Figure 4. Intraurban Transport Eras and Metropolitan Growth Patterns.
  I Walking-Horsecar Era (pre-1850—late 1880s)
  II Electric Streetcar Era (late 1880s—1920)
  III Recreational Automobile Era (1920—1945)
  IV Freeway Era (1945—   )
Source: Adapted from Adams, 1970, p. 56.

the early industrial city. By mid-century most large cities possessed rail suburbs which occupied narrow radial corridors; each contained a linear "rosary bead" settlement pattern of discrete nodes isolated from the city as well as from each other, with walking distance from the railhead determining the extent of local development.

After 1850, following generally discouraging experiments with horse-drawn omnibuses and cable and steam street railways, the horse-drawn streetcar was widely and successfully introduced as a means of intracity transport. Although only slightly faster than pedestrian mobility (up to 5 mph), most cities were able to expand outward to about three miles from downtown thus opening up sizeable new areas for home construction on the urban perimeter. Crosstown lines enabled interstitial as well as radial artery outer city space to develop and the residents of these new horsecar suburbs were able to escape the aging and more crowded housing of the old pedestrian city (Ward, 1971, pp. 128-134). This migration was soon intensified as inner industrial areas expanded and attracted increasing numbers of immigrant working-class families. Since these lower income groups were unable to afford the time and cost of commuting, they could not yet sort themselves into ethnically discrete neighborhoods. The resulting tensions and conflicts quickly spawned a highly stressful inner city social environment, and led to the decentralization of higher income residents; thus was initiated the intraurban geographical stratification and segregation of economic classes, and the American city soon became locked into a residential spatial structure dominated by closed social cells wherein ability to pay and quality of one's lifespace went hand in hand.

Electric Streetcar Era

The localization of middle income groups at the edge of the industrial city was a relatively short-lived phenomenon. By the late 1880s the electric streetcar opened up land for residential development beyond the built-up frontier. During the century's final decade residential suburbia was swiftly transformed from small, exclusive, upper income enclaves into a landscape dominated by middle-class housing tracts. The higher speed of the trolley (15-18 mph) permitted the range of commuting to increase significantly so that the urban development radius could now extend ten miles or more from the city center. In addition to serving new streetcar suburbs, low-fare traction routes quickly blanketed the central city and helped revolutionize its social geography by enabling the residential sorting of the urban population into homogeneous neighborhoods defined by ethnic and income criteria.

The suburbs of the trolley era developed rapidly in a manner consistent with the American rural ideal. The absence of city economic pressures caused by the high cost of land allowed the more lavish use of space, characterized by the lower residential densities associated with the much desired detached single-family house in a garden. Although development stretched several miles out, the trolley lines allowed easy access to the city for the new suburbanites who still depended on the central city for just about everything. Settlement morphology in the streetcar era was dominated by narrow fingerlike linear development which thrust outward from the city along traction routes and their parallel utility service lines. In other axial sectors electrification of railroads and interurbans had permitted more frequent stopping, and the addition of more closely spaced stations saw the older discrete centers coalesce into a continuous corridor. The total urban pattern was one of a distinctly star-shaped metropolis (Figure 4, Era 2) with elongated corridor development in sectors containing public transportation, and empty interstices lying between these radial axes. Local suburban development within streetcar corridors was typified by a continuous strip of largely commercial uses which lined both sides of the tracks. Behind them gridded residential streets paralleled the tracks to a depth of a few blocks on either side; beyond lay open space, often dotted with market gardening farms, which was available to all for recreation.

The values and class consciousness of its steadily expanding middle income population shaped the social geography of streetcar suburbia. Freedom to pursue their own socioeconomic objectives became the hallmark of middle-class families. Such a way of life focused on the narrow, upwardly mobile social interests of the individual family unit hardly contributed to the formation of cohesive stable communities (Yeates and Garner, 1976, p. 191). Frequent upward movement occurred within this society as each salary increase was signified by a move to a "better" neighborhood, and such fine scale residential sifting and sorting produced an internally stratified population spatially segregated according to minor income and status differences. Berry (1973b, pp. 50-51) attributes this growing tie between social and spatial mobility to the drive for achievement, an American cultural dynamic of central importance; thus, the residential location decision, governed by aggressive achievement-oriented behavior, is further expressed in the active defense of one's neighborhood in order to avoid its "downgrading" by the entry of lower status groups. The result was a highly fragmented local population of parochial foci and interests, further abetted by the noncentric physical layout of gridded suburban streets and trolley strip development. What emerged were not "integrated communities arranged about common centers, but a historical and accidental traffic pattern" (Warner, 1962, p. 158).

Important changes in suburban economic geography also occurred in the trolley era. In many of the nation's suburban rail corridors, the onset of urban manufacturing decentralization was giving rise both to reverse commuting and to a growing number of satellite industrial mill and company towns (see Taylor, 1970; Cutler, 1973, pp. 52-57; Buder, 1967). Factories followed the rails outward as they were no longer limited to the central city for assembling raw materials and distributing manufactures; the rising cost of city land, increasing congestion, higher taxes, and nuisance legislation abetted the trend. Although streetcar suburbanization slowed after the turn of the century, a considerable suburban development had been achieved, and it became clear that the burgeoning rail-produced industrial metropolis of the First World War years embodied the spatial transformation of the American city "from the stage of simple urbanism to complex metropolitanism" (Vance, 1964, p. 50).

Recreational Automobile Era

After 1920 the widespread adoption of the private automobile sustained and accentuated the metropolitan trend that slowly turned the city inside out. The rate of suburban population expansion, once and for all, surpassed that of the central city in the twenties (see Kasarda and Redfearn, 1975). By the following decade the suburbs began their domination of metropolitan and national population growth trends (Table 1; Figure 3). A period of great economic prosperity propelled the momentum of mass-scale suburbanization in the 1920s as the national wealth came to be shared by increasing numbers of middle-class Americans. With much satisfaction, these residents of interwar suburbia enjoyed and enhanced the streetcar era improvements in urban life which emphasized solid social identity, family-centered activities, and recreation in the surrounding countryside. Though the Great Depression of the 1930s did slow expansion, its overall impact in the suburbs was much less disastrous than in the cities.

The automobile was the major new spatial force underlying interwar suburban growth. It considerably widened the area of intrametropolitan accessibility and provided greater flexibility and range for locational choices and movement patterns. By opening up unbuilt areas lying between suburban rail axes, the auto quickly lured real estate developers away from older streetcar corridors to the more profitable interstices. The shape of urban development reverted to the circular uniform transport surface pattern (Figure 4, Era 3), as highways built into the interstitial sectors gave rise to a diffuse settlement fabric increasingly dependent on auto mobility. These highways and their new urban bridge and tunnel links were intended as scenic routes for pleasure driving, but the outlying housing tracts they spawned soon converted these parkways into commuter roads. Developers particularly preferred open areas at the urban fringe where large land packages could be easily and cheaply assembled. Quietly subsidizing this kind of suburban growth were federal and state public policies which included financing highway construction, insuring private mortgages, obligating lending institutions to invest heavily in new home building, and later granting low interest loans to special groups such as war veterans. Although this system was popularly hailed as a great success and resulted in widespread economic growth and home ownership, it was not without its detractors. As the fledgling urban planning profession emerged in the interwar years, it judged developers responsible for piecemeal, disorderly growth, unimaginative community design, and the declining level of amenities in the suburban living environment. The critics pointed to the fruits of a modest suburban community planning movement which peaked in the twenties (see Gallion and Eisner, 1975, pp. 127-148), but planned new towns were an idea which never caught on.

The social geography of interwar suburbia was characterized by the intensified residential sorting of groups according to economic status. With the price of housing the filtering mechanism, the new spatial freedom introduced by the automobile permitted ever more widespread segregation among social classes. To ensure the stability of this system, suburban sociospatial partitioning was codified in two ways. Most municipalities quickly adopted newly legitimized zoning regulations to preserve their existing character through control of residential lot and building standards so as to command housing prices consistent with the income and status levels of its residents. Besides these exclusionary economic practices, the widespread use of racial and ethnic "covenants" or deed restrictions enforced local social segregation; these clauses in contracts between developer and home buyer attempted to prevent resale to Jews, blacks, and other minorities, and were highly effective in preserving the white Christian character of nonindustrial suburbs until a 1948 Supreme Court ruling *(Shelley v. Kraemer)* declared the practice unconstitutional and thus unenforceable in the courts.

Led by manufacturing, which by 1920 had seen the rise of major railroad-oriented concentrations of industry at the periphery of large cities, the intraurban deconcentration of economic activity became a recognizable trend during the recreational auto era (Figure 5). Industrial decentralization continued as before and was further aided by the advent of motor trucks, the extension of public utility networks (especially electric power lines) into the newer suburbs, and the gradual shift from vertical to horizontal fabrication methods which require much larger manufacturing sites (see Colby, 1933). As Figure 5 also indicates, the suburbanization of retailing began to occur in the interwar period; however, despite the appearance of the first complete shopping center at outer Kansas City's Country Club Plaza in 1923 (see Wilson, 1974, pp. 43-44) and Sears and Roebuck's opening outlying branches in the 1930s, the suburban retail dominance of the Central Business District (CBD) was not overcome until a decade or more into the postwar era (see Vance, 1962).

Freeway Era

Suburban growth since 1945 has been both swift and massive (Figure 3; Tables 1 and 2). Metropolitan geography in the auto-dominated freeway era has been strongly shaped by new expressways, and resulting accessibility differentials in the urban fringe have again dictated a return to the network-biased metropolis (Figure 4, Era 4). With suburbs spreading in ever-widening arcs since the 1940s, high speed freeways have created a new sense of almost total intrametropolitan flexibility and spatial freedom in the range of locational choices available to a majority

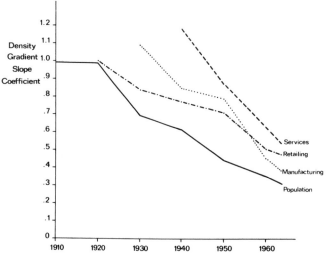

Figure 5. Intrametropolitan Density Gradients, 1910-1963.
Source: Adapted from Mills, 1970, p. 14.

of urban residents. The dramatic upsurge in the postwar deconcentration of nonresidential activities (Figure 5) reveals a similar perception on the part of producers and sellers.

Underlying the massive postwar migration to the outer city were all of the earlier attractions of suburbia, greatly reinforced by the acceleration of dispersive forces. More than a decade's worth of pent-up demand for housing was quickly unleashed in the late forties: potential home owners began to spend freely their considerable personal savings amassed during years of wartime prosperity, and returning servicemen had no trouble securing down payments and mortgages in a time of easy money and ubiquitous government-guaranteed housing loans. The construction industry responded with a prodigious spurt of home building; through mass production techniques, selling prices were kept at modest levels and the housing market attracted all but the lowest income groups. Huge residential developments prevailed: Lakewood Village near Los Angeles accommodated 100,000 and the New York, Pennsylvania, and New Jersey Levittowns were home to almost twice that many (for a close-up look at the last see Gans, 1967).

With the increasing urbanization of the suburbs in the 1960s and 1970s, a transition has been occurring from the city-dominant/suburb-dependent spatial relationship to a far more complex intrametropolitan structure with its urban elements scattered almost randomly within the regional city. In this era of "metropolitan anarchy" (Fagin, 1958) many activities became footloose and could relocate to more desirable sites as situational considerations became less important. Within today's dispersed metropolis, city and suburb have assumed new roles. The central city becomes increasingly specialized as an elitist service center (for those higher order business functions yet unable to deconcentrate) and the home of the metropolitan disadvantaged; the suburbs comprise an expanding band of urban development containing nearly the whole gamut of once exclusively citybound activities. Because of diverging interests and outlooks, deep-seated polarization between city and suburb now prevails. To no small degree this resulted from the accelerated postwar emigration of whites from big cities as an equally rapid influx of blacks replaced them.

Intensified polarization has also affected the organization of social space within suburbia, and its residents increasingly withdraw into insular neighborhoods composed of similar people. This trend is also a result of the recent expansion of the metropolis into an urban whole too vast for personal comprehension. People are reacting by organizing their lives around smaller segments of the outer city which can now satisfy almost every need within a half hour's drive from home. Nowhere is this behavior clearer than in the quintessential suburban city of Los Angeles, where *Sick Cities* author Mitchell Gordon (1971b, p. 23) points out that the whole of L.A. as such has never existed in the minds of its residents, which is the main reason why they and visitors "come away with such sharply divergent, frequently contradictory impressions of the area."

Afterword

This brief historical survey has necessarily been limited to a generalized overview of the geographical sequences of suburban development since 1850. A more detailed map analysis of Chicago's suburban growth (Figure 6) for the same 125-year period, however, shows the broadness of this treatment: suburbanization is revealed as something more complex than a simple outward thrust. We can observe considerable developmental ebb and flow as leapfrogging, backfilling, and frontier stagnation occurred. Nevertheless, good correspondence is seen between the four growth stages and Chicagoland's expansion, and the construct provides a useful general understanding of the spatial dynamics underlying the emergence of modern suburbia.

The overall impression is that the suburban pattern of each of the four eras suggests a continuous spatial trend which has long been characteristic of the American metropolis (see Jackson, 1975). Yet it would be erroneous to conclude that the contemporary urbanization of the suburbs is simply the end product of this century-long evolutionary process.

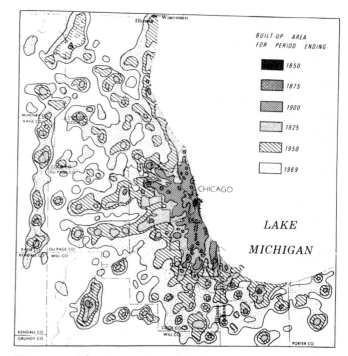

Figure 6. The Expansion of Metropolitan Chicago. Reproduced by permission of the Center for Urban Studies, University of Chicago.

Important new deconcentration forces emerging since 1960 have considerably reinforced and accelerated suburbanization as well as the social and economic abandonment of the central city. We will now focus on this synthesis of old and new forces and the novel spatial patterns that are being forged: the human geography of the current suburban American scene.

II. THE ORGANIZATION OF SUBURBAN SOCIAL SPACE AND ITS HUMAN CONSEQUENCES

... the dominant ethos today is a suburban one. It is as pervasive among minority groups as it is in the society as a whole.

G. Sternlieb

In Chapter I we saw how several interrelated and overlapping forces have shaped the intrametropolitan distribution of population in general and the social geography of the suburbs in particular: (1) the steady decentralization of all but the lowest income groups; (2) the concentration of most new housing at the urban periphery, and lately the increasing agglomeration of commerce and industry in the outer city; (3) the spatial differentiation of metropolitan population along socioeconomic lines which has created considerable variation among communities of different income and social groups; and (4) the continued in-migration of the rural poor to the central cities, a flow which has become predominantly black during the last generation (Danielson, 1972, p. 145). In this chapter contemporary patterns and problems concerning the organization of social space in the outer city will be reviewed. First we will treat the residential spatial structure of suburbia, and then turn to a consideration of the segregation of social groups and its consequences.

Suburban Residential Patterns and Their Interpretation

Although all but the lowest income and certain minority groups have taken advantage of the opportunity to live in the outer city, we have seen that the suburban experience has been a variable one as populations from the beginning have been rigidly stratified in residential space according to their socioeconomic status. At the neighborhood scale, this geographical sorting by class has produced locally homogeneous residential areas which persist with remarkable stability. They continue to attract socially similar newcomers, searching for just such a social niche or community of identity populated by people who share the same attitudes, values, and aspirations. In the overall social mosaic seen at the metropolitan scale, however, heterogeneity dominates the suburban residential map. Income is a most suitable indicator of this social diversity, and the mapping of per capita income at the municipal level in the Philadelphia SMSA (Figure 7) clearly shows the typical socioeconomic smorgasbord encountered in the suburbs of any large city.

Class Divisions in Suburban Social Space

Despite the superficial chaos of the geographically-fragmented pattern observed in Figure 7, it is possible to discern a good degree of spatial order. Berry (1973a, p. 103) suggests the following allocation scheme of the way social classes generally arrange themselves in suburban space. *Upper income* groups cluster in areas possessing both physical isolation and the choicest environmental amenities; *middle income* populations concentrate as closely as possible to the high status residential areas of the most affluent; *moderate income* families eventually occupy the less desirable housing of old industrialized rail corridor towns and the aging innermost suburbs which largely contain multiple dwelling units; and the *low income* and *poor* live in isolation in the decaying centers of old towns and the the dilapidated housing of out-of-the-way poverty pockets. Since desirable and undesirable residential conditions are scattered instead of evenly distributed in geographic space, the considerable socioeconomic balkanization observed in Figure 7 develops as the overall population mosaic is built up.

The residential clustering of income groups of the same level in the Delaware Valley suburbs (Figure 7) is quite consistent with this model: high income regions are localized in areas well endowed with environmental amenities and historical prestige (the well-known Main Line extending west from Philadelphia; Valley Forge; Swarthmore); middle income groups attach themselves to every upper income cluster (particularly north and south of the prestigious Main Line); moderate income suburbanites are concentrated in the aged mill towns of the old Pennsylvania and Reading Railroad corridors which line the Delaware and Schuylkill Rivers (as well as in the farm-dominated exurbs to the far northwest and southeast); and the lowest income

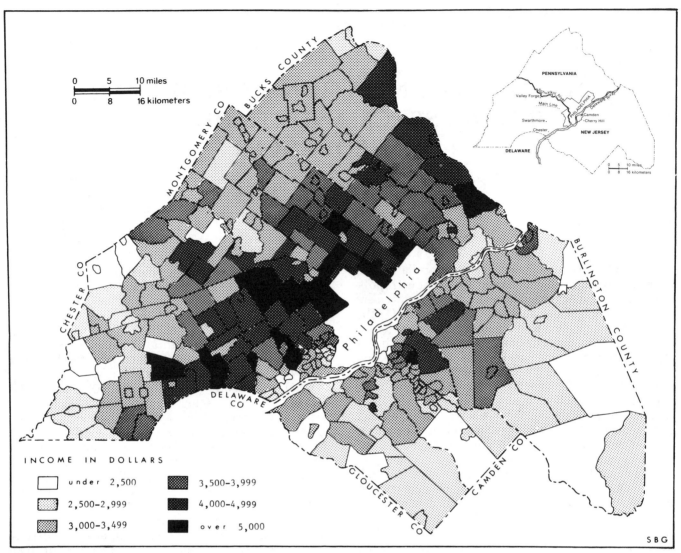

Figure 7. 1970 Per Capita Income by Minor Civil Divisions, Philadelphia SMSA. Reproduced by permission of the Department of Geography, University of North Carolina at Chapel Hill.
Source: Muller, 1974, p. 76.

suburban populations, too thinly spread to be captured at this scale, are tightly clustered in the dying cores of satellite cities (Camden, New Jersey; Chester, Pennsylvania) and many scattered outlying pockets.

Beyond this general model of class segregation, urban geographers have yet to investigate explicitly the processes which have shaped the organization of suburban social space.[4] Extensive research by other social scientists, has established that central city-suburban differences in living patterns are almost entirely accounted for by the different socioeconomic composition of the two populations (National Research Council, 1975, pp. 54-56). Indeed—allowing for the more dispersed settlement fabric, lower residential densities, higher average income, and greater emphasis on class distinctions in suburbia—the social heterogeneity of the suburbs as shown in Figure 7 is quite reminiscent of the central city. Thus we are not dealing with two separate urban worlds, and suburban social patterns can generally be regarded as the most recent manifestation of the overall intraurban residential sorting process.

Traditional income-based class distinctions have become less important in postwar society. Widespread economic prosperity has pushed the entire socioeconomic hierarchy upward, and class strata are now increasingly distinguished by social criteria,

[4] In addition to such major suburban social dimensions as socioeconomic status, ethnicity, and lifestyle, further research is needed on housing provision and maintenance, linkages between community image and residential choice, and the impact of agents such as realtors on information flows affecting intrasuburban migration.

especially lifestyle (Berger, 1960, p. 93). Consequently, the broad income/status partitioning of suburban residential space based exclusively on economic segregation is evolving into a more internally refined sociospatial structure dominated by stratification according to lifestyle. In the 1970s this trend is being hastened and accentuated by the emergence of a new complex of urbanization forces. These are having a considerable impact on the further evolution of residential patterns in metropolitan social space, particularly in suburbia with its more affluent population readily able to act upon new choices vis-a-vis contemporary social trends and lifestyles.

Contemporary Urbanization Influences

Increasing metropolitan scale and population mobility together with declining intraurban population and activity density are the hallmarks of ongoing change within urban America (see Berry, 1973b, pp. 38-48). Underlying these trends is the rise of a new urbanism distinctly different from that of the recent past. Berry (1973b, pp. 48-56) attributes this metamorphosis to a combination of five contemporary urbanization forces: 1) maturation of the postindustrial economy, 2) progressive erosion of core city centrality through intrametropolitan time-space convergence with the improvement of communications technology, 3) the growing linkage between social and spatial mobility, 4) the efficient performance of the suburban housing industry, and 5) emergence of a truly national American society. The first two dimensions relate more to suburban economic geography and will be treated in Chapter III; the last three involve the behavioral and institutional bases of the contemporary organization of suburban social space.

The connection between upward social and spatial mobility has already been mentioned, and is today more apparent than ever. The deeply ingrained cultural drive for achievement requires an aggressive pursuit of higher socioeconomic status. It is expressed spatially by spending one's earnings on the most expensive home affordable in the best possible residential area. Once one attains a higher status mode of living, one joins in vigorous efforts to protect the neighborhood against the entry of status-challenging lower income groups. Should these efforts to defend against the downgrading of the neighborhood fail, one must immediately escape to avoid the social stigma of being identified with the lower status newcomers.

Developers, builders, realtors, and lenders for the past several decades have supported with a high degree of efficiency these desires to maintain suburban segregation according to income and social status. Highly sensitive to market demand conditions, the suburban housing industry, with the approval and financial support of the federal government, has readily and profitably responded by providing a wide variety of spatially discrete homogeneous residential areas catering to the preferences of every class group. Builders particularly have made every effort not to disrupt existing social space patterns. They, like their customers, are constantly reaching upward and seek to construct the highest income housing possible on their development plots. Specializing in giving people what they want, builders are also quick to adapt to changing social trends. Thus today's emphasis on lifestyle and neighborhood image (as shown in the suburban real estate section of any Sunday newspaper) expresses itself in the amenities, housing style, and layout of the total living package offered by major builders to increasingly specialized residential groups.

With the recent emergence of a national American society, segregation of suburban social groups increasingly is being structured at the intermetropolitan scale. Abetted by rising rates of urban population mobility—nearly one fourth of all Americans change their address each year—"archipelagos" of similar suburban communities, with outliers in every metropolis, now extend from coast to coast. Thus families and individuals can easily move and "plug in" again within these sets of interchangeable, nationally-linked residential enclaves with minimal uprooting and disruption of their accustomed living patterns. In fact, real estate consultant services have been specifically created in order to advise relocating companies and people of compatible communities in destination metropolitan areas.

Community Form, the Emerging Mosaic Culture, and Suburban Lifestyles

Collectively these three contemporary urbanization influences—sociospatial mobility, housing industry performance, and the attainment of a national society—have produced a trend toward much more narrowly defined urban communities. In part, this is a reaction against the vast and complex current metropolitan structure whereby people feel it necessary to carve out lesser and more experientially manageable worlds for themselves. More importantly, this trend reflects a powerful need for small-group identity within today's increasingly incomprehensible and tension-ridden society. This urge is expressed spatially by each group's identifying with a specific portion of metropolitan territory, and the resulting rise of a mosaic of such specialized social districts has all but replaced land rent in shaping the morphology of urban settlement (Vance, 1972, pp. 205-210).

The perceived need of individuals to find a refuge from potentially antagonistic rival groups by withdrawing into a territorially-defended enclave inhabited by like-minded persons possessing similar attitudes and goals reinforces the formation of these detached communities of interest and identity. Thus surrounded by formidable social barriers, these self-selected communities have attained a high degree of insularity. The rise of equally limited social networks greatly reduces contact between individuals of different social background; in turn, lack of direct communication among residential groups breeds oversimplified social stereotypes which are legitimized as people start behaving toward each other as if these distorted perceptions were true. This system tends to feed on itself as future mobility then occurs among similarly isolated residential enclaves. At the intermetropolitan level it is already possible "to be a solid citizen of metropolitan New England, San Diego, or Philadelphia and yet be utterly oblivious to the historical cultural identity of those places" (Zelinsky, 1975, p. 112).

Paralleling and complementing this trend toward the territorial detachment of dissimilar social groups is the nationwide emergence of a *mosaic culture*. This consists of a number of subcultures distinguished by sharply contrasting lifestyles which, although divisive for society as a whole, "at another level mutual harmony is produced by mutual withdrawal into homogeneous communities, exclusion and isolation from groups with different life styles and values" (Berry, 1973b, p. 66). The overall reorganization of cultural space is likened by Zelinsky (1975, p. 113) to a multi-layered sandwich composed of strata of varying thicknesses stretching across the country: where a certain stratum or subculture thickens markedly, the dominant group has created a "voluntary region" of its own in that locality. Before turning to the social geography of the mosaic culture we will briefly examine lifestyle itself, which has become the overriding basis of today's class stratification.

Each lifestyle involves a unified group behavior pattern consistent with a central and pervasive life interest, and the lifestyles of each social class can be contrasted according to a number of variables: occupational status, stage in the life cycle, leisure time availability, importance of family versus career objectives, local versus cosmopolitan outlook, and a host of lesser environmental and ecological factors (Feldman and Thielbar, 1975; Bensman and Vidich, 1975). With rising affluence, the lifestyles of all but the underclasses have evolved "in terms of a logic dictated by the values and needs of families in each class as these interact with the increasing resources and possibilities available" (Rainwater, 1975, p. 373). Not surprisingly, as we shall see, lifestyles increasingly vary within classes as suburban living alternatives (condominium apartments, townhouses, retirement communities, etc.) proliferate. This trend is accentuated as the mosaic culture takes root and affiliations with its subcultures intensify. As this occurs, hastened by the persistent unwillingness of different lifestyle groups to share residential space, great numbers of similar people are now congregating in potential communities of every sort. A high degree of satisfaction appears to be widespread as this new social matrix congeals, particularly in the suburbs which to its residents have long been the embodiment of lifestyles desired well before settling there (Hall, 1968, p. 138). Although we need further analysis of the social geography of the suburban mosaic culture, it is possible to delineate and discuss its four major types of lifestyle communities.

The following framework (Berry, 1973b, p. 65; Suttles, 1975, pp. 265-271) can be used to classify these community forms: (1) exclusive suburb/affluent apartment complex concentrations; (2) middle-class family areas; (3) working-class/ethnic-centered/ghetto communities;[5] and (4) cosmopolitan centers. The level of generalization intended is at the scale of what Suttles (1975, pp. 264-265) calls the *minimal named community*, a defended social area equivalent to the suburban housing development or older ethnic colony which is enclosed by popularly recognized neighborhood boundaries. These communities are products of a long pattern of residential segregation and their lifestyles devolve from a fairly uniform population which has faced similar preferences and socioeconomic opportunities; most, however, contain sizeable minorities of residents with varying preferences who do not participate heavily in the locally dominant lifestyle but who tolerate it because little else is available. All four community types are much in evidence in the socially diversifying contemporary suburban scene, and the social geography of each will now be reviewed.

Exclusive Upper Income Suburbs

These high income suburbs are distinguished by exclusive class-reinforcing social interaction. Since houses are built on large properties and screened off by trees and shrubbery, neighboring is physically difficult and people keep in touch by participation in local social networks. The latter are tightly structured around organizations such as churches and country clubs, and newcomers to the community are carefully screened for their social credentials before being accepted. Since many are not accepted, mutually exclusive communication networks can and frequently do develop among affluent groups possessing nearly equally high status (e.g., the ethnic *nouveau riche* and the long-time wealthy Anglo-Saxon Protestant residents). This local social space partitioning can be identified physically in landscape taste and artifact differences (Duncan, 1973). As has been the trend for the last century, most of these detached prestige suburbs are found in the outermost exurban fringes (though notable exceptions do exist in the cases of such elite older inner suburbs as Grosse Pointe, Michigan and Beverly Hills, California) where the settlement pattern is characterized by even more widely spaced housing, quaint classy villages, and semi-rural landscapes dedicated to the "gentleman" farming of fox hunting and horse raising (Hart, 1975, pp. 184-185).

A recent offspring of this elite suburban lifestyle is the growth of luxury apartment complexes which are attracting rising numbers of highly affluent singles,

---

[5] Suburban ghetto communities, whose social interaction patterns are related to those of working-class neighborhoods, will be treated in the following section on the suburbanization of blacks.

families, and senior citizens. Usually operated as condominiums, these swank high rises—veritable vertical country clubs—offer a complete array of first-class services and facilities. Highest status locations are sought out, and the skylines of many a new suburban minicity (for example, International Village in Schaumburg 25 miles northwest of downtown Chicago) and prestigious historical landmark (Valley Forge, Figure 7) have become dominated by these imposing residential structures.

Middle-Class Family Suburbs

The needs and preferences of the nuclear family unit shape the modes of social interaction in middle income areas. The management of children is a central concern, and most local social contact occurs through such family-oriented formal organizations as the PTA, Little League, and the Scouts. Despite the closer spacing of homes and these integrating activities, middle-class suburbanites, like turn-of-the-century streetcar suburbanites are not communally cohesive to any great degree. Emphasis on family privacy and freedom to pursue vigorously its own upwardly mobile aspirations does not encourage the development of extensive local social ties; there is limited and selective neighboring (mostly child-related), and even socializing with relatives is infrequent. Most social interaction revolves around a non-local network of self-selected friends widely distributed in suburban space. The insular single-family house and dependence on the automobile for all tripmaking accommodate these preferences, and foster a strong matching or *congruence* between lifestyle and the spatial arrangement of the residential environment (Michelson, 1976, pp. 26-27, 79-87).

The long-standing casualness of local social involvement by future-oriented middle income families assumes a central role in the emerging community forms of the mosaic culture. The widely dispersed lifespaces of middle-class suburbanites, who increasingly participate in social networks which function with little regard for distance or territoriality, typify the unhitching of communities from geographically-fixed localities (see Webber, 1968). As this kind of spatial behavior proliferates, much suburban social activity occurs beyond the local neighborhood. Thus, the territorial community has been eclipsed by the community of interest formed through voluntary association. For the suburban resident these dispersed social networks now comprise macrocommunities of metropolitanwide dimensions. Yet in spite of the recent expansion of macrocommunities of interest, the larger societal trends toward narrower defended residential enclaves and intensifying subcultural affiliation have given rise to microcommunities which are equally important for understanding the social geography of middle income family areas.

The contemporary microcommunity may be defined as "an instrument of environmental control requiring a rather low level of contact" (National Research Council, 1975, p. 71). Well suited to the upwardly mobile behavior of middle-class residential areas, these "communities of limited liability" require only a minimum of local group activity (see Suttles, 1972, pp. 44-81). This largely involves social mobilization for defending the neighborhood territory when it appears to be threatened. Microcommunities, as secure residential havens worthy of individual social and property investment, expect their inhabitants to defend local social space, provide good will, and evince predictable behavior. On the other hand, families may leave on short notice should the opportunity arise for a move to a "better" neighborhood.

As was the case with elite upper income suburbs, middle income family areas are also accommodating alternative lifestyles as multiple-dwelling housing rapidly expands. Propelled by skyrocketing land and building costs, suburban apartment construction doubled during the 1960s to more than six million units nationwide; in the same period suburbia's proportion of total SMSA multiple-unit dwellings rose from 22 to 33 percent; and by 1972 more suburban apartment than detached housing units were being started. Besides lower upkeep costs, the new multi-unit lifestyle attracts middle income suburbanites for the same reason as their wealthier counterparts: the need for less space in an era of smaller families and working wives, extra services such as tennis courts and swimming pools, and a full array of social facilities. Although the rise of apartment living has altered the physical character of many residential areas, its social impact has been to reinforce rather than diminish class segregation within the suburban socioeconomic mosaic: the income and status levels of apartment buyers and renters are quite similar to those of surrounding neighborhoods which often supply many of the new multiple-unit dwellers (Dingemans, 1975a).

Apartment-based lifestyles support and are being supported by the growing trend away from nuclear family childraising as the special residential character of middle income suburbs. The postwar suburban generation is producing a steadily rising number of young people and childless couples who require smaller living quarters and who prefer to reside in the same social setting they were raised in. Apartment living is also increasingly attractive to single persons (a group which owns more than five million suburban houses), who have already organized intricate social networks and voluntary regions of their own throughout suburbia. In addition, the "empty nester" households of older couples whose children have left home require less living space and this group's continued preference for socioeconomically similar neighborhoods further accentuates the demand for more suburban apartment housing.

Working-Class Suburbs

Suburban working-class neighborhoods have

steadily multiplied since the end of World War Two. Before 1945 they were confined mainly to narrow factory town rail sectors (in which they still predominate), but with increased auto ownership and prosperity moderate income blue-collar families have begun to disperse from industrial corridors and peripheral central city neighborhoods. Though by no means able to penetrate affluent residential areas, working-class families have moved into many modestly priced suburban housing tracts (often near newly dispersed manufacturing facilities) as well as to the innermost suburbs whose older attached housing filtered down to those spilling across the city line.

Unlike the carefully structured modes of socializing in middle-class macro- and microcommunities, working-class ethnic-centered neighborhoods are characterized by a broad social interaction of informal groups congregating at such local meeting places as the church, tavern, street corner, or door stoop. Local group acceptance and integration is the dominant social value, and communal life stresses the availability of a satisfying peer group society, similar neighbors, maintaining easy access among people well known to each other, and collective defense of neighborhood respectability (see Rainwater, 1966, pp. 24-25; Michelson, 1976, pp. 66-71). Thus, much tighter local social cohesion and control dominates suburban working-class neighborhoods. Moreover, local area attachment is reinforced by a person-oriented rather than a material- or achievement-oriented outlook: working-class suburbanites have no great hopes of getting ahead in their largely blue-collar jobs, have few aspirations vis-a-vis upward social mobility, and therefore view their present home and community as a place of permanent settlement (Berger, 1971, p. 169).

Working-class lifestyles are most congruent with high-density residential environments which facilitate the intensive use of outdoor space for local social interaction. This need for a low degree of spatial separation between people explains the continuing affinity of these groups for older factory town rail corridors which contain most of suburbia's moderately priced attached housing. The physical and social character of these working-class communities, which Lieberson (1962) found to be virtually identical to blue-collar central city neighborhoods, offsets them sharply from surrounding higher income suburbs. The outdoor street life focus is the opposite of middle-class family areas which emphasize the privacy of the detached house. Residents of working-class neighborhoods tend to economize on housing to spend their modest incomes on other needs and interests; thus, while home interiors are meticulously well kept, neighborhood appearance is a low priority concern and accounts for the frequent unattractiveness of these communities. Social network patterns are also quite different: whereas middle-class suburbs stress the nuclear family unit, socialization with friends, and a minimum of local contact, working-class neighborhoods accentuate the extended family, frequent home entertaining of relatives rather than acquaintances, and a great deal of informal local social interaction outside the home.

A more socially ambitious upper stratum of the suburban working class has been emerging outside of these factory town enclaves since the 1940s and lately shows signs of making the transition to lower-middle-class lifestyles. Understandably, the upward passage of this group is marked by the acquisition of new behavior patterns as well as the retention of some old ones. The working class has always had its more ambitious sector of strivers willing to get ahead by forsaking traditional communities and lifestyles. Through hard work and careful saving these families have managed to buy their own homes in lower-middle income areas. Once settled, a perception of residential permanency again takes over: the family is fully satisfied that it has "finally made it" and any remaining aspirations are transferred to the children who will continue to advance via higher education. As a result, these newer working-class suburbs have become quite stable; for example Levittown, Pennsylvania, near U.S. Steel's Fairless Works just northeast of Philadelphia, still contains well over 25 percent of its original 1952 residents (Bittan, 1972, p. 80). Also promoting the stability of these residential areas is the in-migration of extended family members of the earlier settlers, as later emigrants from traditional working-class communities first come to know through frequent visits and then prefer the immediate vicinities of their relatives' homes.

Working-class residents of lower-middle-class family areas tend to adopt many of the customs and attitudes of their neighborhood. They desire detached houses; prefer home owning to renting; seek to obtain appliances and creature comforts; keep up the house exterior and yard as well as the indoors; and practice selective neighboring. But at the same time many of the old ways persist. Extended family visiting dominates social interaction; they participate minimally in formal groups; and they live very much in the present and with little class consciousness (see Dobriner, 1963, pp. 57-59).

Because there has been little research on the subject, we know relatively little about suburban ethnicity and its spatial structure. Undoubtedly, the ethnic consciousness movement of the 1970s has been widely felt in suburbia and is an additional source of its intensifying social fragmentation. Because of their long stability and similarity to blue-collar central city neighborhoods, traditional suburban working-class communities are likely to be centers of strong ethnic identification. Particularly where traditional ethnic kinship structure diverges from the American nuclear family norm—such as extended family households containing several unmarried adult male relatives—detached dwelling family areas do not favor such old-fashioned working-class living arrangements not only because of strong local disapproval but also because government home loan guarantee policies overwhelmingly favor single-family houses (Hahn, 1973). Ethnic concentrations are also proliferating in suburban sectors outside factory town corridors. We have already noted the geographical tendency of non-traditional upper level working-class groups to cluster around their relatives' homes. These kinds of migratory ties also appear to be widespread among certain middle income ethnic groups, and in the Philadelphia suburbs, perhaps because of the need to minimize distance to few existing houses of worship, Jews, Ukrainians, and Greeks have often preferred to stick together with fellow ethnics in their upward social and spatial mobility.

Suburban Cosmopolitan Centers

Cosmopolites are talented, well-educated persons with broad national rather than narrow local horizons; they judge people and situations liberally according to objective criteria; and they participate in far-flung intra- and intermetropolitan social networks and communities of interest (see Michelson, 1976, pp. 87-91). Professionals, intellectuals, students, artists, writers, and mutually tolerated misfits who are spatially oriented to the high culture life of the metropolis inhabit cosmopolitan neighborhoods. As theaters, concert facilities, fine restaurants, and other such cultural activities continue to deconcentrate from the central city's downtown, cosmopolitan centers are now spreading throughout suburbia. To be sure, suburbanites have always heavily supported center city cultural events by supplying large audiences (as in the case of New York's theaters, symphonies and opera companies) and crucial financing (Main Line matrons and the Philadelphia Orchestra). And the suburbs have also been havens for talented artists (New York's periodic exurbia of the central Hudson Valley, easternmost Long Island, and upper Bucks County in nearby Pennsylvania).

The new suburban cosmopolitan community, however, is a contemporary phenomenon and involves the voluntary residential congregation of people of similar interests in their own social district. University suburbs, which already contain a critical mass of cosmopolites, are particularly favored and, more often than not, towns such as Ann Arbor, Boulder, and Princeton provide a cultural life almost as rich as that of their nearby central cities. College communities themselves are rapidly proliferating in the outer city as a number of downtown universities are successfully decentralizing some of their educational programs to suburban branch campuses. In addition to their usual college-age populations, these branches are also serving local demands for continuing education. The nation's most respected adult education facility, New York's New School for Social Research, opened its first suburban outlet in Westchester County in February 1976. Besides its recent growth in college towns, the cosmopolitan lifestyle is also attracted to the vicinities of prestigious new suburban culture centers (e.g., the Wolf Trap Farm Park music-dance-theater complex in Vienna, Virginia outside Washington, D.C.) which are springing up in every region of the country.

The Intensifying Heterogeneity of Suburban Society

As the mosaic culture matures, those living in its new community forms appear satisfied. More than ever before, individuals and families are able to select both the lifestyle most suited to their preferences and a corresponding suburban social district which best caters to their specific needs and interests. Easy mobility within the mosaic enhances its attractiveness, and the increasing predilection of younger people to pick up and discard lifestyles at will augurs for continuing subcultural fragmentation in the future (see Rainwater, 1975). Yet while the mosaic culture promises further heterogeneity, its recently emerged communities are firmly established and will anchor the suburban societal fabric of the late twentieth century. Socioeconomic persistence has long characterized most suburban residential areas (see Farley, 1964), and it is likely that even less neighborhood turnover will occur in the future. With the exception of old rail corridors and aging inner suburbs bordering the central city, downward filtering of housing does not occur widely in the outer city. If anything, middle and upper income neighborhoods built since 1945 are now appreciating in value. This housing trend is greatly reinforced by continuing inflation and is rapidly putting a new home beyond the financial means of all but the most affluent (Sternlieb, 1972; Breckenfeld, 1976).

Although most individuals and families enjoy the many advantages of living in the mosaic culture, their mutual withdrawal into tightly-knit interest groups and insulated residential enclaves is divisive for suburban society as a whole. Sharply defined cleavages in social interaction reflect spatial incompatibility among contemporary suburban lifestyles and their corresponding communities. The intensifying fragmentation of social space buttresses duplication of function within an exceedingly compartmentalized suburban land use pattern which caters to each income and subcultural group, and encourages decreasing participation in the larger society. Schaeffer and Sclar (1975, p. 119) capture the essence of the sociospatial *status quo*:

> With massive auto transportation, people have found a way to isolate themselves; a way to avoid confrontation; a way to privacy among their peer group.... they have stratified the urban landscape like a checker board, here a piece for the young married, there one for health care, here one for shopping, there one for the swinging jet set, here one for industry, there one for the aged, here one for the rich in their fifties, there a ghetto for the *Untermensch*—be they poor or racially despised. When people move from square to square, they move purposefully, determinedly.... They see nothing except what they are determined to see. Everything else is shut out from their experience.

The Segregation of Suburban Social Groups

The segregation of subcultural communities in contemporary social space appears to be intensifying. The social districts are carefully delimited with a pervasive spirit of every-group-for-itself, and they defend their territory against outside challengers or those who might threaten their social and economic status. The social barricades are unsubtle—palisade fences, guarded gates, and other "keep out" landscape symbols (Clay, 1973, pp. 162-175)—as the groups consciously wall themselves off from each other. The resulting isolation promotes tertiary interaction, i.e, the groups behave toward one another as if the mass media stereotypes were true.

Affluent residents of comfortable neighborhoods may express satisfaction with the present conditions of suburban social segregation. This is not the case with many disadvantaged groups who constitute increasingly important elements in urban social geography. One major disadvantaged group, suburban blacks,[6] have encountered social barriers in the outer city to such an extent that their resulting social isolation and spatial segregation is perhaps the most pronounced pattern on suburbia's residential map.

There is a deeply imbedded and pervasive racial segregation within the fragmented social geography of the outer city. Whereas blacks comprise 11 percent of the total U.S. population and 12 percent of its metropolitan residents, they account for less than five percent of the nation's suburbanites. We will examine this sociospatial racial cleavage according to its historical trends, contemporary spatial forms, perpetuation mechanisms, and human consequences.

Black Suburbanization Trends

Twentieth-century black suburbanization trends (Figure 8) reveal that such popular suburban epithets as "lily white" and "white noose" have some factual basis. It would certainly not be an overstatement to claim that blacks largely have been denied entrance to the suburbs. Prewar patterns are insignificant since comparatively few blacks lived in the North, but postwar trends clearly show a rapidly widening divergence of whites and blacks in the suburbs. Both graphs in Figure 8 indicate a stable black suburban population over recent decades. A large proportion of this population still inhabits tiny, widely dispersed, and highly segregated traditionally black areas with settlement histories of five decades or more. In some instances, large enclaves of similar age are present in satellite towns adjacent to large central cities, i.e., Evanston, Illinois; Pasadena, California; and Mount Vernon, New York. Together, these black suburbs have accounted for a stable three percent of the total population in the outer rings of non-Southern SMSAs since the 1920s (Farley, 1970, pp. 513-514). The modest postwar growth of black suburbs has intensified residential densities within these older pockets. Very recently, however, black

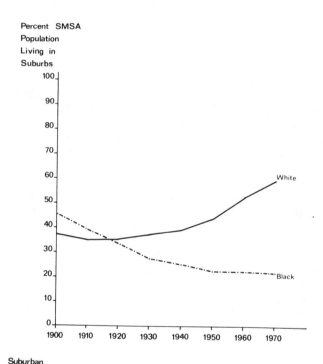

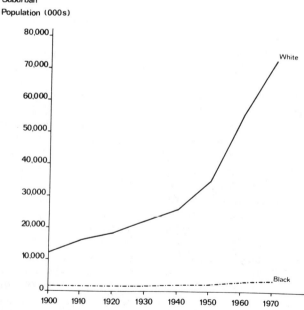

Figure 8 (a and b). Black Suburbanization Trends, 1900–1970.

---

[6] Apart from blacks, other disadvantaged suburban groups now beginning to receive attention are the poor and the elderly (see Masotti and Hadden, 1974, pp. 212-222, 253-259). The 1970 census revealed that 21 percent of the poor (vs. 30 percent in the central cities) and 21.5 percent of the elderly live in the suburban rings of the nation's SMSAs. Although often discussed in local and regional transportation, housing, and other plans, the geographical problems of suburbia's youth, women, handicapped, and other less privileged groups have yet to be considered systematically. The mobility problems of all of the above-mentioned groups, with some emphasis on the suburbs, are reviewed in Muller (1975).

population increases have also resulted from selective expansion of central city ghettos into contiguous inner suburbs—a potentially significant trend for future suburban social geography.

An overview of the latest census data indicates that America's suburbs remain all but closed to blacks. During the 1960s the percentage of blacks in the suburban population of SMSAs (as defined in 1970) increased imperceptibly from 4.78 to 4.82. Although 800,000 blacks did enter suburbia in the sixties, their gains were all but obliterated by the more than 15.5 million whites who constituted 95 percent of the decade's new suburban migrants.

Viewed from the slightly different perspective of the total black population itself, census findings are similar. From 1960 to 1970 the percentage of this group residing in the suburbs increased only from 15.1 to 16.2 percent, compared to the 35.4 to 40.4 percent rise for whites; in terms of percentage increases whites (+14 percent) again led blacks (+7.2 percent) by a wide margin. By region, the West (25.6 to 29.5 percent), North Central (11.6 to 12.8 percent), and South (14.2 to 14.8 percent) gained in black suburban population, whereas the Northeast held a constant 18.7 percent (Pendleton, 1973, p. 173). On the other hand, black concentration in central cities during the sixties increased notably (52.8 to 58.0 percent) at a time when the corresponding white population declined (from 31.5 to 27.8 percent).

Because of the much smaller absolute number of suburban blacks in the 1960 base data—2.8 million to 56.3 million whites—suburbanization rates during the 1960s are deceptive (29 percent growth for blacks, 28 percent for whites). Nevertheless every region recorded modest black gains except the South, where overall black suburban population declined from 12.6 to 10.3 percent. This trend must be balanced against the conclusive findings of a study undertaken by the Federal Reserve Bank of Boston (Glantz and Delaney, 1973) indicating that black suburbanization in the sixties did not result in any meaningful progress toward racial integration. Specifically, this study concluded that: (1) there was very little change in the distribution of blacks both between and within central cities and suburbs during the 1960s; (2) new suburban black migrants were moving overwhelmingly into widely scattered already-black neighborhoods with almost no penetration of white residential areas; and (3) despite small absolute and proportionate nonwhite suburban SMSA increases from 1960 to 1970, intermunicipal segregation in the decade actually increased by an average of 15 percent in 14 large SMSAs surveyed.[7]

[7] These included all of the eleven largest SMSAs (cf. Table 2) except Washington, D.C., plus Dallas, Atlanta, Birmingham, and Greensboro-Winston Salem-High Point. Only New York City and Los Angeles recorded decreases, and suburban Chicago, Detroit, Baltimore, Dallas, Atlanta, and Birmingham all recorded intermunicipal segregation index increases in excess of 20 percent.

Thus, in the 1970s suburbia remains largely off-limits to nonwhites. And for those blacks who do manage to enter the few relatively undesirable suburban neighborhoods abandoned to them by whites, "it has meant little more than exchanging one hand-me-down neighborhood for another," as improvement in the quality of life over the inner city ghetto is usually negligible (Delaney, 1974a, p. 278). Before treating this restricted suburban access of higher income nonwhites, we will discuss the two varieties of black suburbs which have emerged.

Black Suburban Settlement Types

Spatial patterns of black suburban settlement are intricately tied to the urban ghettoization process which concentrates blacks in a limited number of residential areas (to the extent that they dominate neighborhoods in excess of fifty percent of the total population). These are sealed off, surrounded by powerful social barriers maintained through constant external pressures. Rose (1972) has classified these outlying racial concentrations into two distinct spatial forms: *colonized* and *ghettoized* black suburban enclaves (Figure 9).

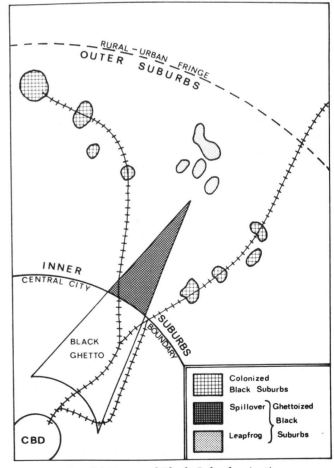

Figure 9. Spatial Forms of Black Suburbanization.
Source: Adapted from Rose, 1972, p. 408.

Colonized black communities tend to be small stable pockets which have persisted for several decades originating as "shacktowns" on the then rural-urban fringe.[8] In the Northeast these congregations are commonly attached to old rail corridors, such as suburban Philadelphia's Main Line, and are direct descendants of the nineteenth-century servants' quarters, usually relegated to undesirable trackside locations, which housed the domestic employees of wealthy landowners of the period. Always segregated, these low income black colonies have become completely isolated by the social barriers erected as modern suburban development engulfed them. Kinloch, Missouri (discussed in detail by Ernst, 1976) just outside St. Louis is typical:

> It is a desperately poor community surrounded by affluent white suburbs. Kinloch's single-family homes are in various stages of deterioration; its streets are largely unpaved; and at the same time it has the highest rate of school taxes in the county, the lowest tax base, and the worst schools. Kinloch survives as a community simply because no other area is willing to absorb it and its problems. Meanwhile everything is done to isolate the black suburb from its wealthier neighbors. Roads from the next community actually stop one foot before Kinloch's borders, and while a full-scale wall like that in Berlin has not been constructed around the community, the northern community of Berkeley has built a chain-link fence all along Kinloch's border (Palen, 1975, p. 175).

Although most colonized black suburbs are characterized by aged, dilapidated housing, stagnant or declining low income populations, and a deteriorating quality of life, there are a few exceptions. One is Glenarden in Prince Georges County, Maryland, just northeast of the District of Columbia. Here local black political control enabled annexation of nearby unbuilt land for development in detached and garden apartment dwellings which have attracted hundreds of middle income families. Another is Hollydale, Ohio, northwest of Cincinnati, which has had similar success as a new outlier of the older adjacent Woodlawn-Lincoln Heights colony. A third exception is Lawnside, New Jersey, southeast of Philadelphia, which has maintained a staunchly independent middle-class black population for over a century and has recently added new housing by developing previously bypassed residentially-zoned properties.

Since World War Two *ghettoized* black suburbanization commonly has been of the spillover type. This results from a sectoral expansion of the central city ghetto across city lines into adjacent suburban territory (Figure 9). As poorest blacks are forced to abandon unlivable dwellings at the inner edge of the ghetto, they move outward to the nearest available housing. This housing in turn has been abandoned by less poor blacks seeking better housing in outer ghetto neighborhoods. The more favorable residential environment of the inner suburban margins of the advancing black community has attracted a middle-class population of better-educated, young black families. This spillover process is well-advanced in many cities, such as Cleveland, St. Louis, Washington, D.C., Chicago, Atlanta, Miami, Los Angeles, and parts of the New York metropolis (the last documented in Sternlieb and Beaton, 1972).

The other form of ghettoized suburb is the *leapfrog* type, most often an exclave located beyond the spillover ghetto (Figure 9). This is a newly emerging phenomenon, and Rose (1972, pp. 411-414) has identified three such clusters in central Long Island, as well as a fourth in East Palo Alto, California. These black pockets are relatively undesirable residential areas and almost always consist of deteriorating, cheaply constructed early postwar tract housing which whites have abandoned (see Kaplan, 1976b, pp. 28-30).

Mechanisms Perpetuating Suburban Racial Segregation

Thus suburban blacks live in residential areas which are quite different from those occupied by whites. Even when blacks are able to find suburban housing outside of their colonized and ghettoized enclaves, they tend to be tightly segregated at the block level. A tally (by the author) of such microscale 1970 census data for the suburban component of the Philadelphia Urbanized Area using all census tracts containing seemingly integrated black proportions of 17.5 to 50 percent, showed that no less than 52 percent of 1600 blocks surveyed were completely white whereas 59 percent of the remaining black-occupied blocks possessed ghetto-like concentrations of 50 percent black or higher. A comparison of housing conditions in suburban black neighborhoods reveals further disparities: blacks own fewer dwellings (50.2 to 67.8 percent) whose standards and values are significantly lower ($16,430 or 65 percent of the $25,087 white 1970 average) (Pendleton, 1973, pp. 180-181). On the whole there are far fewer blacks in the suburbs than are warranted by this group's rising income levels, and the consensus among researchers in the mid-seventies is that the root cause of this residential segregation by race has been and continues to be not class difference but private and public discrimination (this argument is summarized by Taeuber, 1975, esp. pp. 90-92). The *de facto* dual housing market and *de jure* exclusionary zoning mechanisms which perpetuate suburban racial segregation merit closer examination.

The Suburban Dual Housing Market and Its Impact

White reluctance to share residential space with

---

[8] Ward (1971, p. 142) points out that the original nucleus of black central city ghettos was often an inner suburban locality in the late nineteenth-century metropolis. Rooming and lodging houses built by the rich were taken over and soon became overcrowded deteriorating residential areas. New York City's Harlem best exemplifies this type of ghetto development.

blacks has nurtured a discriminatory dualistic housing market which systematically excludes nonwhites and preserves the racial segregation of the suburbs.[9] *Subdivision developers* regularly attempted to influence the social composition of their housing tracts via restrictive covenants and other screening devices. Levitt, for example, was well known for personally scrutinizing his buyers in order to keep out "undesirable class and racial groups." *Realtors* carefully screen potential home buyers and usually "steer" whites to one listing of houses for sale and blacks to another (a more sophisticated suburban cousin of cruder central city "blockbusting" and other panic-selling techniques). Although one can assign the primary responsibility to the real estate industry for perpetuating segregation by steering blacks away from white areas, its agents, as local businessmen, feel they have little choice but to cater to the social preferences of their communities. *Lending institutions*, through spatially discriminating methods of "redlining," financially support the stability of a chosen set of residential areas. In addition, by denying mortgage and home improvement loans, they allow the ensuing self-destructive disinvestment process to ruin whole non-favored neighborhoods. Until the early 1960s the *federal government* encouraged and heavily subsidized policies creating white suburbs and black central cities by explicitly forbidding home construction loans which fostered racial integration. The Federal Housing Administration practiced redlining and the agency's handbooks prior to the Kennedy administration specifically warned against the "infiltration of inharmonious racial groups" and "the presence of incompatible racial elements." Since the early sixties, the federal government has implicitly fostered segregation by neglecting to enforce newly enacted fair housing and other equal opportunity legislation. *Local government* zealously uses its land control powers to enforce exclusionary zoning ordinances (a subject to be discussed in the following section). Many suburban municipalities even try to destroy their black communities by rezoning them commercial or industrial, or to isolate them totally by surrounding them with noxious, nonresidential "no-man" zones (Kaplan, 1976b, pp. 27-28). By continuing to tolerate without widespread protest this entrenched system of unequal treatment, *society* gives every indication of satisfaction with the *status quo*.

Ironically, the failure of recent attempts to reduce racial inequality in shopping for suburban housing comes at a time of steady expansion for the black middle class and its supposed ability to buy its way into good quality residential areas. Although largely denied access to the suburban housing market, middle-class blacks, like other groups before them who have achieved this level of socioeconomic status, are congregating in the best peripheral neighborhoods available in order to maintain social distance from lower income nonwhite inner city neighborhoods from which they may have recently emigrated. Masotti and Hadden (1974, pp. 80-81, 280-281) include examples of this behavior. With the concentration of an increasing number of upwardly mobile middle income blacks at the outer edge of the spillover ghetto (Figure 9), the demand for better housing exerts pressures to widen the inner suburban foothold. Shunning both militancy and publicity, those behind these efforts probe until the least resistant surrounding racial barriers begin to yield. Once a breach occurs, word rapidly diffuses through the black community and the new residential pocket is quickly filled. However, this only amounts to a temporary relaxation in the high pressures of "pent up" demand, as there is only a tightly limited supply of good suburban housing available to blacks at any one time.

These efforts aimed at enlarging the black suburban presence notwithstanding, the results are hardly noticeable when we consider 1960-1970 census change data. Berry (1975) underscores the ineffectiveness of suburban integration attempts in the 1960s by analyzing the Chicagoland dual housing market which, it is fair to say, is quite typical of conditions prevailing in the other large metropolitan regions. During the boom period of the sixties—a time when accelerated downward filtering of housing enabled nonwhites to gain access to many decent quality outer neighborhoods in the central city—the black proportion of families migrating to the Chicago suburbs was only 4.6 percent; when dwelling unit data are considered, the black share of newly constructed suburban houses (1.9 percent) and apartments (3.3 percent) was even lower. With the recent recession and dramatic decline of housing starts in the midseventies, prospects for immediate improvement of this situation are remote.

White Resistance to Suburban Integration

White resistance to the suburbanization of blacks is universal. Skin color is a "master statusdetermining trait," and white suburbanites at every income level perceive blacks as a threat to their own social status (Berry et al., 1976b, esp. pp. 246-260). In order to protect their status, whites must avoid sharing residential space with blacks and must preserve geographical separation of the races.

Low and moderate income suburban workingclass neighborhoods are especially blunt in their hostility toward nonwhites. The lack of upward mobility aspirations found in these communities reinforces neighborhood attachment and the desire to maintain an image of respectability, thus eliciting a

---

[9] Berry (1975) discusses these market mechanisms and their spatial consequences in detail; he defines (p. 169) a dualistic housing market as "one in which there is residential segregation by race, and in which a white majority preempts the outlying areas of new construction and existing zones of superior residential amenity, while the black minority is left the existing housing stock, usually within the central city, and frequently in the zones of greatest environmental risk."

passionate defense of the neighborhood. Vandalism and even full-scale rioting often accompany attempts by pioneering black families to penetrate these white communities whose unity is often accentuated by tight ethnic clannishness. Upper income residential suburbs handle similar conflicts in a more refined but just as effective manner, usually through adroit maneuvering by sellers and realtors. Consider the response of the affluent Main Line district west of Philadelphia to a recent Pennsylvania fair housing law designed to curb excesses in the state's real estate industry: in the first year following implementation of this legislation nearly two thirds of local house turnovers were transacted privately without any official involvement of a realtor, and the social *status quo* of this wealthy area remained unaffected (Kron, 1973). There is also intense resistance to black entry into acutely class-conscious, upwardly mobile middle-class suburbs, particularly since social status is almost always derived from the externally perceived image of one's neighborhood. Only in a very few middle income suburbs is there even reluctant acceptance of a limited number of black households, which results in "salt-and-pepper" integration—insignificant sprinklings of blacks here and there—frequently characterized by the "Ralph Bunche syndrome" of welcoming one respectable black family to the street but not two or more (Delaney, 1974a, pp. 279-280).

Some proponents of suburban integration are seizing upon this entrée into certain "liberal" middle income suburban communities by attempting to devise programs for the orderly influx of more blacks while preventing the flight of white residents common in situations of rapid neighborhood racial change. The belief underlying these schemes is that whites might well wish to remain in a community if firm assurances can be given that the entry of blacks will be controlled so as to guarantee a large local white majority. At issue is the size of the critical mass of black immigrants or the *tipping point*, purported to be in the 20 to 30 percent range, beyond which whites pull out and the entire neighborhood rapidly turns all black. The inner middle-class Chicago suburb of Oak Park recently has been attempting to draw up this kind of "social compact" ordinance whereby a maximum of 30 percent black population would be mandated (Farrell, 1974). Prior to 1974 only two percent of Oak Park's residents were nonwhite. Local fear of an imminent spillover from the adjacent Austin neighborhood—the leading edge of Chicago's expanding West Side ghetto—and the subsequent likelihood of black "flooding" followed by white abandonment, has prompted Oak Park to explore the controversial black quota solution. Although it is too soon to tell if such a scheme can work to integrate a large suburban community, the initial results have not been productive. So far, blacks have been segregated within Oak Park and are heavily concentrated in neighborhoods bordering the city line which directly face the Austin ghetto; the community remains "redlined" (Kaplan, 1976b, pp. 32-33). Nonacceptance of the social compact idea has been widespread, especially in black quarters where several community leaders have been particularly outspoken in their opposition to the quota concept. As a result the quota has been tabled, and a policy of selective discrimination prevails (Berry *et al.*, 1976b, p. 238).

Rising Black Frustration

The immovability of suburban racial barriers is now resulting in such rising black frustration that nonwhite pressures to enter suburbia are declining in many metropolitan areas. Endless obstacles thrown up by dual housing market mechanisms have greatly increased black cynicism in the 1970s. Nonwhite realtors and those sympathetic to minorities are almost always kept from membership on suburban real estate boards and therefore from access to better house listings. Black home-seekers are constantly reminded of racial discrimination in newspaper advertisements containing such wording as "exclusive," "secluded and private," and "country club," which are interpreted as cues that minorities are unwelcome (Outtz, 1974). Nonwhite buyers are seldom given a chance to negotiate or "sleep" on a price without having a house suddenly disappear from the market. When they are able to enter a newly opened suburban area, middle-class blacks are often forced to share residential space with socially dissimilar lower income blacks, thus considerably reducing perceived levels of neighborhood quality (Caldwell, 1974; also see Willie, 1975). Despite ongoing attempts to modify these conditions, little change is taking place because

> ... by preventing the minority person from being able to shop for housing in the way that is normal for his white peers, a permanent barrier to residential desegregation has been created which may be beyond the power of positive law to reach (J. H. Denton as quoted by Foley, 1975, p. 174).

With heightened black suburban disillusionment in the 1970s has come an intensified aversion to "pioneering" formerly all white areas, always a distressing practice involving exposure to white hostility and frequently physical violence. In a mid-sixties study of suburbs outside Seattle, Norwood and Barth (1972, pp. 118-123) concluded optimistically that initial opposition to blacks might subside over time. They even proposed a multi-stage assimilation model (pre-entry, entry, accommodation) leading toward residential integration. However, a newer analysis of the Philadelphia suburbs by Cottingham (1975, esp. pp. 277, 281) paints a more accurate picture of the contemporary metropolitan reality. She finds an increasing reluctance among central city blacks—regardless of income level—to move beyond their established neighborhoods. In particular, avoidance of white suburbia is reflected in consistently low black suburbanization rates: three percent for all blacks vs. 32 percent for nonblacks, and six percent for upper income blacks vs. 57 percent for affluent whites in the 1965–1970 period.

Exclusionary Zoning and the Persistence of Closed Suburbs

Exclusionary zoning is a legal impediment which powerfully reinforces the racial barriers encountered by blacks seeking access to housing in the outer city. It has enabled the suburban municipality, through local land control powers, to enforce various ordinances which guarantee that the sale and rental prices of properties are not affordable by low and moderate income individuals of any social group.

In Chapter I we saw that the historical roots of suburban exclusionism extend back at least as far as the late nineteenth century. The desires of the newly emerging (and suburbanizing) middle class to maintain social distance from the immigrant underclass of the inner city were quickly expressed in an abiding concern with defending newly-won suburban territory against all outside challengers of lower social status. In the 1920s zoning reinforced this exclusionism because property owners in the automobile suburbs clearly recognized it as an effective weapon for preserving single-family housing, suburban neighborhood character, and the existing class structure. Thus,

> Instead of becoming a useful tool for the rational ordering of land in metropolitan areas, zoning became a way for suburbs to pirate from the city only its desirable functions and residents. Suburban governments became like so many residential hotels, fighting for the upper-income trade while trying to force the deadbeats to go elsewhere (Jackson, 1973, p. 210).

Although now stripped of some of its most discriminatory excesses,[10] the exclusionary system, institutionalized in almost every community through suburbia's fragmented local governmental structure, has persisted essentially unchanged since zoning was first widely introduced after World War One. Current exclusionary zoning practices (reviewed by Rubinowitz, 1974, pp. 27–44; and Fried, 1972, pp. 41–49) assume a variety of forms, the general thrust of which overwhelmingly favors expensive one-family homes on large lots, thus pricing out and defending against nonaffluent populations. The number and location of multiple-family units, if permitted at all, are tightly controlled by piecemeal zoning. This practice limits land parcel size in order to prevent construction of large apartment complexes by assigning sites next to obnoxious land uses, which usually deters builders, and by restricting apartment size, which hold the school-age population down ("hysterectomy" zoning). Other less costly housing, especially mobile homes, is almost universally banned in middle and upper income suburbs.[11] Municipalities justify large-lot zoning of one half-acre or more as a way to control local growth, preserve low population densities and good environmental quality, and avoid urban problems which emanate from "overcrowded" conditions. Moreover, most municipalities also enforce housing codes whose standards are so high (and so costly to meet for building permit approval) that critics refer to them as "Cadillac" requirements. Among these are extravagant structural and material stipulations, lavish minimum floor space requirements, and sidewalk and sewer tie-in regulations. Although many communities recognize that their zoning and building ordinances result in an exclusively middle and upper income local population, they argue that preservation of the municipal tax structure would be impossible if lower income housing were suddenly permitted because of the huge burden that such an influx of people would place upon social and other public services.

The results of half a century of suburban exclusion are increasingly evident. 1970 census data on metropolitan housing available to low and moderate income groups reveal a striking disparity between central city and suburbia: for owner-occupied homes valued at less than $12,500 the city proportion (31.2 percent) was almost double that of the suburbs (17.6 percent), and for rentals of less than $80 per month the differential (23.8 vs. 13.7 percent) was almost identical (Downs, 1973, pp. 191–192). The outlook for narrowing this divergence is not promising when one considers zoning data on undeveloped suburban land. The metropolitan New York case is typical. In 1971 Davidoff et al. (1974, p. 136) observed that: 90 percent of the remaining open residential land within the New York state suburbs was zoned for single-family homes; in northern New Jersey 82 percent of such land was zoned for half-acre or larger lots; and in southwestern Connecticut at least 75 percent of the available land was zoned for lots of an acre or more. Suburban Philadelphia is similar: 64 percent of developable residential land is zoned for one acre or larger lots (with one third exceeding two acres), 38 percent of suburban municipalities prohibit multiple-family housing, and 42 percent of those that permit such housing restrict the number of bedrooms per apartment unit (Anastasia, 1975).

Perhaps the most telling impact of exclusion in recent years is the inevitable overall suburban housing shortage caused by artificial limitations on dwell-

---

[10] Although the 1948 Supreme Court decision in the case of *Shelley v. Kraemer* removed the courts from enforcing restrictive ethnic and racial covenants, it did not outlaw the practice. According to Foley (1975, pp. 172–173) these deed restrictions are still widespread and often may be used by realtors and sellers as unofficial guides in the transfer of residential properties.

[11] Despite exclusion from higher status residential areas, mobile home parks have grown steadily around lower income suburbs. These types of suburban dwellings doubled in number during the 1960s and continue to proliferate as attractive housing alternatives for moderate income groups.

ing unit supply. Zoning thus greatly reinforces the upward spiral of both land and home construction costs, so much so that middle income groups are increasingly unable to compete in certain segments of the suburban housing market at the present time. In the early seventies, only 20 percent of all the families residing in the New York metropolis could afford a new house; significantly, this proportion would rise to 47.5 percent if suburban zoning were to change and 57.5 percent if mobile homes were more widely permitted (Caldwell, 1973, p. 19). As shown earlier, recession and high mortgage interest rates through the mid-1970s have almost certainly combined to erode further the financial position of middle income households. Even such mass builders as Levitt and Sons claimed in 1975 that they could not sell a new house to families earning under $17,000 annually. In some suburban communities this new reality is finally raising doubts as to the long-run effects of the exclusionary system. The concern, however, is not for disadvantaged outsiders but is one of self-interest: residents are becoming aware that the expense of local housing is forcing out their own elderly and young married populations. Thus limited, moderate income, multiple-unit housing plans are tolerated in a growing number of suburban municipalities, but almost always on the condition that eligibility be restricted to senior citizens and others already living in the community.

The Continuing Legal Struggle Against Suburban Exclusion

To the American public at large exclusionary zoning is most widely known as a term referring to the ongoing legal battle to break the economic segregation system of the nation's suburbs (for a general review of this movement, its attendant issues, and important legal decisions through the early seventies see *Newsweek*, 1971; Babcock, 1973; Masotti and Hadden, 1974, pp. 112-175; and Platt, 1976, pp. 20-23).

Through the mid-sixties legal decisions on local zoning strongly supported suburban exclusionism. Since zoning originated from enabling acts passed by state legislatures, cases were usually confined to the state courts. Federal courts rarely heard such cases; the U.S. Supreme Court has not ruled on municipal zoning since it approved this method of local land use control in 1926, and still refuses to hear such cases a half-century later. In recent years, however, the growing financial commitment of the federal government to local planning and community development (an outcome of wide-ranging social legislation passed by Congress since 1963) has increased the involvement of the federal judiciary in exclusion cases. At the same time, the legal record has become less one-sided as certain decisions have been rendered in favor of opening the suburbs to lower income populations. As yet many legal con-

traditions remain to be resolved. Opponents of exclusionary zoning have gained mostly moral victories to date, and the closed suburban system persists. Rather than review the full record of exclusionary zoning adjudication since 1960,[12] let us briefly examine four cases of the mid-seventies which are pertinent to the future of present forms of suburban exclusionism: (1) Mount Laurel Township, New Jersey, (2) Petaluma, California, (3) metropolitan Hartford, Connecticut, and (4) metropolitan Chicago.

Mount Laurel, New Jersey

The Mount Laurel, New Jersey case (Anastasia, 1975; Trillin, 1976) involves the most important state-level decision yet rendered, and deals not only with the narrow question of restrictive municipal zoning but also the wider issue of how local government may use its powers to shape the socioeconomic composition of its community. Ruling in March 1975 on Mount Laurel's township ordinances which banned apartments and single-family homes on lots smaller than a quarter-acre, the New Jersey Supreme Court struck down exclusionary zoning statewide. The Court felt that restrictive zoning went beyond the powers that the state legislature had intended to give local governments, and directed that every such municipality must change its land use regulations to "make available an appropriate variety of choice in housing." More importantly, the Court also found that any developing community shares with its neighbors a legal and social obligation to provide a fair share of housing for low and moderate income families. Thus a New Jersey municipality now has a regional responsibility for people living outside its boundaries, and may no longer enforce local housing plans which operate exclusively for the financial advantage of its taxpaying residents.

The Mount Laurel decision was upheld in October 1975 by the U.S. Supreme Court, which refused to hear this appealed case based exclusively on state law. Courts in other states are bound to be influenced and may well be persuaded to take a more active role and render similar verdicts. Yet in realistic terms Mount Laurel is a hollow victory and will hardly result in meaningful immediate change. Whereas New Jersey law now states that lower income housing is required, public funds are not available to subsidize its building, an absolute necessity since this type of suburban construction is a money-losing proposition for private builders.

Petaluma, California

The recently resolved legal conflict over zoning in the outer San Francisco suburb of Petaluma (Fosburgh, 1975) centered around a municipality's right

---

[12] Harvey (1972, pp. 21-24) has done much of this in an earlier Resource Paper.

to determine the need to slow its own growth, and act accordingly by sharply limiting the supply of new housing for nonresidents. A local zoning ordinance restricted new housing to only 500 units annually for five years in order to "shape orderly growth" and safeguard the "small town character" of the community. A coalition of builder organizations initiated the Petaluma case in 1972 after the ordinance was approved in a local referendum; since the lawsuit was brought on constitutional grounds it was pursued in the federal courts. In January 1974 the U.S. District Court of San Francisco ruled in favor of the plaintiffs and declared the ordinance unconstitutional because it abridged the Fourteenth Amendment equal-protection-under-the-law provision by denying citizens the right "to travel and to settle wherever they wished." On first appeal, however, the U.S. Appellate Court in August 1975 overturned the lower court ruling and let the original ordinance stand on the ground that Petaluma's "public welfare" as a community overrode the more general societal right to travel. By deciding on final appeal to refuse to intervene in the case on February 23, 1976, the United States Supreme Court upheld the appellate court decision and legitimized this use of zoning to limit new housing.

Although the Petaluma case was essentially an environmental clash between builder and conservationist interests, the final court decision was significant because it appears to remove a community's obligation to provide for regional housing needs in planning its future development. By further restricting supply, the cost of housing in Petaluma will become that much higher and effectively exclude all but the affluent. Moreover, scores of other suburban communities watched the case with interest and many in California are now following suit by implementing their own "grow slow" zoning ordinances (Jensen, 1976).

Hartford and Its Suburbs

The growing federal involvement in the legal struggle to open the suburbs is underlined in the case of Hartford, Connecticut and its suburbs (Fellows, 1975, 1976). In September 1975, the central city successfully obtained a federal district court injunction to prevent payment of more than $4 million in community development funds which had been awarded to seven suburban towns by the U.S. Department of Housing and Urban Development. Hartford's lawsuit claimed that 90 percent of the metropolitan poor were concentrated within its boundaries and that these federal funds should therefore be used to relieve some of that city's heavy regional burden of housing and to provide social services for low income families (the suburbs intended to use this federal aid for building new sewers, road, and parks). The local U.S. District Court sided with Hartford in January 1976 by making the original temporary injunction permanent, but on the narrow ground that HUD violated the federal Community Development Act of 1974 by waiving application requirements on projections of low income population growth in the suburban communities. The waiver was permitted by HUD because appropriate data were difficult to obtain, a liberty the court refused to sanction since the 1974 law "clearly states, as one of its objectives, the spatial deconcentration of lower income groups, particularly from the central cities" (Fellows, 1976, p. 58).

Since HUD was processing at least 3000 applications for community development assistance from all parts of the United States in the fall of 1975, many of them involving similar city-suburb competition, the Connecticut decision may have wide impact. However, as one judge in the Hartford case conceded, the communities involved were eligible to reapply for the same funding provided they attached the necessary low income projections, and some of these suburban municipalities have indeed done so after making the required revisions in their applications.

Metropolitan Chicago

The increasing federal presence and the widening of the legal movement to open the suburbs through nonzoning cases is further demonstrated in the U.S. Supreme Court's decision of April 20, 1976 in *Hills v. Gautreaux* (Farrell, 1976). The black plaintiffs had brought suit against HUD and the Chicago Housing Authority in 1966 on the ground that the agencies, by restricting construction of low-cost housing almost exclusively to black inner city neighborhoods, had perpetuated racial segregation in that city. The unanimous Supreme Court ruling in the Gautreaux case agreed that this government confinement policy violated the constitutional rights of blacks, and affirmed that federal courts can order HUD to locate subsidized low income housing in white suburbs to relieve urban racial segregation. HUD had argued that it had no authority to interfere in local government affairs by locating public housing in suburban communities, especially when the latter had not been found guilty of practicing racial or economic discrimination. The high court, rejecting the notion that the central city-suburb border is a barrier to remedies for segregation, maintained that HUD could intervene because suburban municipalities were still free to exercise fully their local land control powers through zoning.

The last qualification allows each suburb to block low income housing, and therefore renders the Gautreaux case but another hollow victory which is unlikely to open the suburbs in the near future. HUD cannot require suburbs to accept low-cost housing, and the burden of proof still rests with the litigant to show that the federal government has practiced discriminatory use of housing subsidy monies (Oser, 1976). Thus the question of suburbia's regional role in sharing in the solution of central city problems is still unresolved. Emotions run high because suburbs wish to preserve the present character of their neighborhoods. As a result a growing number of suburban municipalities are foregoing application for large sums of federal community development aid which is contingent upon planning for local low-cost housing (a few of Hartford's suburban communities chose not to reapply for federal funds rather than prepare low income population projections). One danger inherent in the widening suburban nonparticipation in federal housing programs is that large cities may be the ultimate losers, because if the suburbs no longer apply, their congressmen (who constitute a sizeable voting bloc in the House) will increasingly vote not to appropriate community development funds.

* * *

Although the Mount Laurel, Petaluma, Hartford, and Chicago cases represent the latest confrontations in the continuing legal struggle against suburban exclusionism, no clear pattern has emerged from these decisions. The refusal of the U.S. Supreme Court to consider Mount Laurel's final appeal confines exclusionary zoning matters to the state courts for the foreseeable future. Thus this major legal conflict is certain to continue in the absence of a landmark court ruling, and the issue of open versus closed suburbs is likely to remain one of the nation's leading metropolitan crises for some time to come.

The Failure of Housing Programs to Open the Suburbs

As the legal struggle over exclusionism has intensified since the late 1960s, a simultaneous movement involving local housing programs to open the suburbs voluntarily has been under way in certain urban areas. At the state level, Massachusetts and New York have been prominent; the former has endorsed mixed income publicly subsidized housing projects, as well as a 1969 "anti-snob" zoning law which aims at a one-tenth low income dwelling proportion in new developments; and the latter has developed an ambitious plan for massive aid to open wealthy Westchester County through the state's Urban Development Corporation. Metropolitan-level programs have also been announced, with some modest initial successes recently reported for Minneapolis–St. Paul, Indianapolis, and Washington D.C.'s Maryland suburbs. Although planning strategies abound (see as an example Downs, 1973), these and other less publicized efforts for reducing suburban economic segregation have been isolated and in the aggregate have accomplished very little. After five years under the new zoning law, almost no progress has been made in Massachusetts' suburbs toward meeting lower income housing goals. And in New York the much heralded Westchester campaign was abruptly cancelled in 1973 in face of that county's overwhelming opposition.

The most advanced open housing plan of the 1970s has been implemented in metropolitan Dayton (Gruen and Gruen, 1972). This "fair share" plan was adopted in 1970 when, under the aegis of the Miami Valley Regional Planning Commission, the area's suburban municipalities reluctantly agreed to accept certain percentages of low and moderate income housing. By the end of 1974 more than half of the planned 14,000 residential units were open and occupied by lower income families who had relocated from Dayton. These housing developments, widely scattered across many outlying communities, were given such typically suburban names as "Chevy Chase Village" and "Northlake Hills," and consist of a number of garden apartment complexes. As might be expected there was considerable local resistance to the newcomers (Delaney, 1974b), and although many were enthusiastic about the extra living space, good schools and recreational facilities, they were also bewildered by their new surroundings and the challenge of adjusting to them. Of particular concern were fear of going out at night, the absence of city-style social services, and mobility problems (public transportation was found to be useless and total reliance on the automobile was an experience new to most). Although long-time suburban residents have expressed surprise that their new neighbors appear to be taking good care of their properties and that only a small minority are black, there is much resentment and total avoidance of social contact with the lower status newcomers.

By the mid-seventies it had become evident that such housing programs were not succeeding in opening the nation's suburbs to lower income groups, a conclusion endorsed by a late-1975 conference of leading urbanologists at the Center for the Study of Democratic Institutions (Lindsey, 1975b). Failure to increase the access of low and moderate income families to suburbia was attributed to: the unremitting resistance of middle and upper income communities whose residents feared property value losses, erosion of suburban lifesyles, and the proliferation of violent crime and other serious urban problems; recent government actions and court decisions which allow exclusionism to persist; and the policies of the Nixon and Ford administrations which have practically eliminated lower income housing subsidies. Moreover, the recent spread of the grassroots "slow growth" movement combined with rapidly rising construction and land costs has exacerbated the shortage of affordable housing for all but the most affluent. These forces have accentuated greatly the already formidable economic barriers encountered by the central city underclass seeking to enter the suburbs. Looking ahead, the conferees were pessimistic that meaningful progress toward open housing could be achieved in the foreseeable future, and based what little optimism they had upon vague hopes of massive new federal aid combined with the development of more effective instruments of metropolitan government.

Human Consequences of Suburban Exclusionism

Contemporary trends in intraurban social geography, dominated by intensifying residential affiliation with the detached communities of the mosaic culture, are strengthening economic barriers against lower income housing in the suburbs. For blacks, this suburban filter is doubly effective since racial rather than economic segregation is mainly responsible for the exclusion of nonwhites from the outer city. Suburban exclusionism in one form or another will persist, and its present and future consequences need to be weighed.

The Spatial Mismatch of Employment and Housing

The growing geographical disparity between employment and housing within the contemporary metropolis (see Chapter III) has now reached crisis proportions (for a discussion of pertinent issues see: Gold, 1972; Cox, 1973, pp. 62-66; Masotti and Hadden, 1974, pp. 311-318; Christian, 1975). The blue-collar jobs most compatible with the limited education and skills of low and moderate income central city residents are precisely those which are suburbanizing the fastest without commensurate growth of replacement jobs in the city. Thus, with a rapidly shrinking employment base for workers with modest skills in the central city's economy, those jobs which have traditionally served as points of entry into the metropolitan labor force for the unskilled are simply disappearing.

Residential adjustment by this central city population to the dispersing job market is prevented largely by suburban housing barriers. A double standard prevails in the outer city, where municipalities want high tax-ratable industries but not their lower income work force. The Princeton, New Jersey vicinity is typical: the *Wall Street Journal* reports that the surrounding 400 square mile area contains land zoned for an additional 1.2 million manufacturing and research jobs, but only enough residentially zoned land to house 144,000 more workers (Harvey, 1972, p. 22). As a result, blue-collar city laborers must commute longer distances to keep up with the widening separation between residence and workplace. This is mirrored in the steady rise of reverse commuting which nearly doubled in the largest SMSAs during the 1960s, and the trend has almost certainly continued unabated since. Nonwhites seem to be especially affected: a recent study (McKay, 1973) based on data from six large SMSAs showed that the black inner city rate of suburban commuting was fully 40 percent higher than that for whites.

Reverse commuting inconveniences abound. As trip lengths increase so do the money and time costs of the daily work journey. In many urban areas these costs have become so restrictive that they foster absenteeism. High job turnover rates also result, and in many metropolises the job retention rate following city-to-suburb relocation is as low as ten percent. Moreover, there is usually little incentive to engage in reverse commuting since no opportunity to improve one's job status is involved; in other words, the same central city job offers the same meager financial reward but now requires a more burdensome work trip. Mobility problems also aggravate metropolitan spatial injustices for low and moderate income city residents, particularly blacks (see Rabin, 1973). These groups own far fewer automobiles, a critical factor since more than 90 percent of all suburban travel is by car. Because universally inadequate public transporation in the suburbs is accessible to only a tiny fraction of dispersed expressway-oriented employers, non-car-owning transit riders find job opportunities drastically limited in the outer city.

Despite these serious movement constraints, better transportation access to the suburban labor market is not the answer to improving the underemployment situation of inner city workers. Recent studies (e.g., Bederman and Adams, 1974) have demonstrated that journey to work is hardly the most important problem faced by lower income central city residents. Rather, other obstacles to employment must be overcome, such as generally low and weakly marketable skill levels, a deficiency most correctable by intensive and widespread job training programs, and racial and other biases in hiring practices (see Masters, 1975). Although specific research on dualistic job markets has yet to be undertaken, there is little doubt that as job opportunities suburbanize, residential and employment discrimination become mutually reinforcing (National Research Council, 1975, pp. 21-29). Also more important than transportation constraints are communication barriers which impede central city residents seeking work in the suburbs: information flows on job openings are almost always restricted to suburban newspapers and employment agencies, and job searches in suburbia are virtually impossible without an automobile. Overall, the multiplicity of these hindrances amounts to considerable inequality in access to suburban job opportunities. As a result, a growing number of otherwise employable city residents simply give up; and if present trends persist, inner city blue-collar neighborhoods are certain to become expanding areas of chronic unemployment.

Other Consequences

A whole array of secondary impacts flows from the tightening residential concentration of lower income groups in general, and blacks in particular, in the nation's central cities (see Cox, 1973, pp. 59-62; Rubinowitz, 1974, pp. 18-25).

There are strong indications today that the trends identified in the late-1960s report of the President's Commission on Crimes of Violence have not been redirected and are indeed now producing the anticipated further metropolitan social fragmentation, heightened segregation by class and race and polarization of attitudes on an increasing variety of urban issues. Moreover, the persistent lack of freedom of residential choice by minorities and the central city underclass who cannot meet the standards of the suburban filter means, in effect, that the outer ring of the metropolis is dictating living conditions to the inner. What is beginning to emerge is the form of metropolitan social organization which the National Advisory (Kerner) Commission on Civil Disorders foresaw in 1968:

> ... [an overall] trend toward predominantly black cities surrounded by almost entirely white suburbs—the geographic manifestation of "two nations, one black and one white, separate and unequal".... Within two decades [of the mid-1960s] this division could be so deep that it would be almost impossible to unite ... [and would entail] a conclusive repudiation of the traditional American ideals of individual dignity, freedom, and equality of opportunity.

In a current interview (U.S.N.W.R., 1976) Roy Wilkins, executive director of the NAACP, stated that we are now headed for a (largely nonviolent) racial showdown because change for the better in housing, jobs, income, and education is coming too slowly for the younger black generation.

Increasing black loss of faith in the system is occurring despite the spillover suburbanization of middle-class blacks in certain metropolitan areas. As we have seen, racial change here is not accompanied by the lowering of housing barriers between whites and blacks. George Sternlieb (U.S.N.W.R., 1971, p. 45), a leading student of the inner suburban zone of emergence, puts it this way:

> The prime question which is not being approached in our day is this: Will this old suburb serve as a satisfactory safety valve for the [black] guy or will it over a period of time convince him that all this business of trying to make it in America really doesn't work? I am afraid that the odds right now are on the latter.

A corollary of this trend is the crucial implication it has for the fate of the central city: with all but complete white middle-class abandonment, the problem of retaining the middle income black in the city may eventually loom large because the only thing keeping him there now is that there is no better outer residential area available to him.

There is little doubt that growing racial and economic polarization is both persistently self-reinforcing and intensifying as the deconcentration of urban activities proceeds apace in the 1970s (Rabin, 1973, p. 64).

III. THE NEW ROLE OF THE SUBURBS IN METROPOLITAN ECONOMIC GEOGRAPHY

> *Regional centers have turned into minicities . . . The result has been a little-remarked but momentous change in urban geography. The economic magnetism of the great centers has split asunder the functions of most large cities . . . Instead of a single nucleus there are several: the old downtown and a band of satellite centers on the periphery.*
>
> G. Breckenfeld

Because changing sociospatial forces continue to modify the suburban residential mosaic, we must examine processes which are dispersing economic activity in order to understand the locational dynamics of the contemporary restructuring of intrametropolitan space and the growing dominance of the outer city. The suburbanization of commerce and industry, underway for the first two thirds of this century, has accelerated strikingly since the mid-sixties, and its intensification in the 1970s has reshaped the economic geography of the metropolis. Retailing and the rapid rise of the catalytic regional shopping center led this latest and most vigorous episode of intraurban activity deconcentration. Following close behind was the dramatic upsurge in the suburbanization of employment, not only in manufacturing but increasingly in office-based tertiary, quaternary, and quinary functions.[13] Originally content to locate at any interchange or other site convenient to the expressway network, suburban economic activities are now gravitating toward each other. Accordingly, multi-functional urban cores (minicities) have emerged swiftly in the outer city, and these major nodes are now beginning to confer a greater degree of spatial order on the heretofore centerless distribution of production in the suburbs. This chapter will trace the individual paths whereby retailing and employment have dispersed through the outer city since 1960, the formation of minicities and their impact on suburban spatial organization, and the consequences of these structural changes for intrametropolitan economic geography.

The Decentralization of Retailing

The intraurban decentralization of retailing began after World War Two, as shown by its density gradient measure which fell by more than 50 percent in the 1945-1963 period alone (Figure 5). More recent data for the 15 largest metropolitan areas (Table 3, Columns 3-4) indicate a further acceleration of the deconcentration trend: from 1963 to 1972 the suburban ring's share of total SMSA retail sales rose from 48.5 to 65 percent.

The expansion of postwar suburban retailing is really the story of the arrival and diffusion of the large shopping center. In the late forties and early fifties outlying retail centers spread slowly, particularly in the older metropolitan areas of the North and East, as consumer and retailer ties to the CBD were relinquished reluctantly. During those years only modest-sized neighborhood and community shopping centers appeared. However, once the break with downtown was made by 1960, the much larger scale regional center quickly came to dominate suburban retailing. The diffusion of the planned regional shopping center (exceeding 300,000 square feet of sales area on a site of at least 30 acres) has been traced by Cohen (1972), and shows a rising growth trend beginning in 1955 and turning sharply upward in 1959 to be sustained through his data cutoff in 1968. The rapid takeoff at the end of the 1950s coincides with the shift from the *consequent* to the *catalytic* stage of shopping center evolution (Epstein, 1967), i.e. the transition from stores passively following decentralizing population to the dynamic leadership of center developers in actively shaping the growth of the outer suburbs by attracting people and other activities to locate around their new malls.

The consequent stage of retail deconcentration (1945-1960) entailed the leisurely outward drift of stores in the wake of suburban residential development. The pronounced reluctance of retailers to move large stores into the suburbs characterized this period. The continuing success of downtown stores did not immediately require testing the unknown waters beyond the city line. Mass merchandising concepts themselves were relatively new in early postwar America, and the large chains wanted more experience in refining such selling approaches at established city locations before undertaking major commitments in the untried suburban market. As a

---

[13] Tertiary economic activity involves services of all kinds; quaternary functions entail the collection, processing, and distribution of information; quinary producers engage in control activities.

Table 3. SELECTED DATA ON THE DECONCENTRATION OF INTRAMETROPOLITAN ECONOMIC ACTIVITY IN THE FIFTEEN LARGEST SMSAs

SMSA	Percent Suburban Share Total Jobs		Percent Suburban Share Total SMSA Retail Sales		Percent Suburban Share Total SMSA Manufacturing Employment	
	1960	1970	1963	1972	1963	1972
New York	28.8	35.9	32.9	N.A.	19.1	53.4
Los Angeles*	47.8	54.3	58.7	60.0	63.9	64.0
Chicago	32.2	47.5	43.1	56.8	41.0	57.4
Philadelphia	37.0	51.8	56.6	66.7	50.5	59.3
Detroit	43.3	61.4	57.3	74.1	59.3	67.6
San Francisco	44.9	50.0	52.0	63.3	53.3	62.3
Washington DC	36.2	54.9	57.9	76.3	55.8	64.7
Boston	55.5	62.2	68.8	76.3	71.8	78.2
Pittsburgh	64.0	63.7	65.9	77.0	70.0	76.1
St. Louis	39.3	58.0	62.5	77.2	50.3	62.0
Baltimore	34.1	49.9	41.9	61.5	45.4	68.3
Cleveland	28.3	46.0	45.2	69.0	39.7	51.3
Houston*	15.7	24.4	17.6	29.0	28.8	34.3
Minneapolis-St. Paul	23.6	41.1	38.5	62.9	32.7	45.3
Dallas*	24.4	29.0	28.8	58.6	21.2	53.6
Average	37.0	47.6	48.5	64.9	46.8	59.9

* Annexation of suburban territory since 1960.
Sources: Rosenthal (1974b); 1963 Census of Business; 1972 Censuses of Retail Trade and Manufacturing.

result, through the late fifties most outlying retail centers were small isolated clusters of moderate order convenience goods establishments interspersed with a few widely scattered concentrations of high order shoppers goods stores.[14] The typical commercial development of this period was a highway-oriented grouping of retail facilities usually strung out haphazardly along major arteries leading out of the city. In the absence of serious competition from the major chains, local retailers thrived on these highway strips where the formula for success involved little more than a main road location, a saleable product, and free parking at the front door.

Although small shopping centers and commercial strips dominated, innovative consequent era developers began to achieve success with their relatively few regional centers built in the inner suburbs before 1955 (prototypes such as Boston's Shoppers World, Chicago's Evergreen Plaza, and Los Angeles' Lakewood). This message, however, spread very slowly in the 1950s as "safe" market development strategies prevailed and big suburban stores were opened only after an outlying area was settled and threshold demands were comfortably surpassed.[15] Cautious retailing did not dissipate until the early 1960s when the long learning process about suburban market size and tastes came to an end, and the sustained growth of large outlying regional centers finally began.

The shift to the catalytic stage of retail decentralization was accomplished swiftly after 1960 with the recognition of the full economic potential of the suburban marketplace, increasingly settled by the more affluent segments of the metropolitan population. Steadily rising real incomes, triggered by the booming aerospace-led economy of the mid- and late sixties, created a virtually insatiable suburban demand for durable consumer goods. With almost no preexisting retail facilities in the burgeoning outer suburbs, regional shopping centers quickly sprang up at the most accessible highway junction locations.

The catalytic strategy was very successful and most new malls became magnetic attractions in their suburban sectors. Typical of this new growth pole function was the Rouse Corporation's large suburban Philadelphia shopping facility at what is now Cherry Hill, New Jersey, which opened in 1961 and im-

---

[14] The order of a good is its spatial range or the distance that consumers are willing to travel to purchase it; a hierarchy of such ranges exists so that higher order goods draw customers from wider surrounding areas than do lower order goods. Low order convenience goods are everyday items such as food, newspapers, and gasoline which are in frequent demand; high order shoppers goods are expensive items such as furniture, major appliances, and automobiles, which are demanded less frequently and involve comparison shopping.

[15] The threshold demand is the minimum number of potential customers residing within the spatial range of a retail good to enable the sale of that good at a profit.

mediately drew large crowds of shoppers as well as the attention of sightseers and developers throughout the Northeast. Locally, Cherry Hill Mall sparked the rapid urban growth of South Jersey and provided a much needed focus for this otherwise sprawling residential area; in fact, the surrounding community was so impressed that its citizens voted to rename their municipality in honor of the new shopping center. Through widely repeated expressions of this sort, suburban residents were signalling their growing perception of new shopping malls as prestige-laden places. These sentiments were not lost upon commercial developers, who by the end of the 1960s were openly capitalizing on the now glamorous images projected by suburban retail nodes.

These developers preferred larger sites in the more distant suburbs, not only to take advantage of lower land costs but also to resist encroachment by parasitic discount houses and other highway strip facilities which had by now gravitated to roadsides leading to regional centers in the older inner suburbs. Huge parking lots as well as a number of architectural and atmospheric innovations (more important location factors than shopping trip length in the all but frictionless freeway metropolis) were introduced in the fierce competition to lure shoppers from ever widening suburban tributary areas. Inevitably, mall size itself became a primary attractive force. No longer content to merely repeat the familiar dual anchor department stores/air conditioned enclosed two-level mall (first innovated at Victor Gruen's Southdale center outside Minneapolis in 1956), shopping center developers by 1970 had significantly broadened both the scale and range of functions of their facilities and in the process helped revolutionize the geography of the outer city.

The Superregional Mall of the 1970s

These efforts culminated in the emergence of the superregional mall in the early 1970s, an innovation still sweeping the nation's suburbs (Morris, 1969; Breckenfeld, 1972; U.S.N.W.R., 1973; King 1974). Woodfield Mall in suburban Schaumburg, Illinois just northwest of Chicago's O'Hare International Airport, is the world's largest. Its vital statistics underscore the grandiose scale of such contemporary retail facilities: four huge anchor department stores and 230 smaller shops which occupy more than 2.2 million square feet on three levels; 10,800 parking spaces and over 100,000 visitors daily; and an annual sales volume between $150 and $200 million.

The shopping center of the 1970s can also be distinguished from its forerunners by a subtle but critical shift in primary emphasis from mass selling to serving a much wider spectrum of the needs of suburbanites. Today's malls have become convenient all-purpose places to go: after home and work they are now the third most popular place for spending one's time in the suburbs. Many observers view the superregional center as the outer city equivalent of downtown (see Breckenfeld, 1972) and increasingly describe it by using such terms as "acropolis" and "piazza." This transformation of the mall into a "recreational shopping park" (Berry et al., 1976a, p. 46) is endorsed by Woodfield's promotions director:

> We encourage housewives to come out and shop, have lunch, have their hair done, see a movie, shop some more, then meet their husbands after work for dinner—to spend their entire day here, in other words. (U.S.N.W.R., 1973, p. 46)

The new "hub" function is reflected in the myriad activities now found at malls throughout the nation, among them symphony concerts, religious services, political rallies, live theater, and psychological counseling. Perhaps the most far-reaching of the nonretailing functions has been the recent emergence of shopping centers as social focal points in suburbia. Long favored as informal gathering places, particularly by less mobile suburban teenagers and the elderly, large malls now show signs of becoming true community centers for their surrounding residential areas. Although badly needed activity space and time budget studies have not yet been conducted, there is much circumstantial evidence to suggest that suburbanites are increasingly structuring their lives around the centers. To many residents of the outer city the regional mall provides a symbol of identity as well as a sense of community, a seemingly logical outcome in their search for roots in the otherwise geographically disorganized suburban environment which has grown up so rapidly in the postwar era.

Undeniably, the trend toward larger regional shopping malls has been one of the most spectacular successes in American suburban history: mall sales doubled in the 1965-1973 period and the nation's 15,000 plus shopping centers now account for well over 50 percent of total U.S. annual retail sales. Although the superregional mall is still diffusing across the country and many older centers are still adding new stores, doubts are now arising as to how much longer the supersize retailing phenomenon can continue. For one thing, three-level facilities such as Woodfield and suburban San Jose's Eastridge reach the upper size limit which commercial developers acknowledge as the equivalent of a three city-block walk. Moreover, huge suburban sites of one hundred acres or more are no longer cheaply or easily assembled, and construction costs for giant malls now exceed $100 million. The uncertain energy situation now makes building in the far metropolitan fringes (most other suburban markets are by now saturated with regional centers) a much riskier economic proposition than it was a few years ago. Finally, the federal Environmental Protection Agency and local governments are increasingly taking developers to task for the pollution caused by large new centers and the spontaneous adjoining growth they trigger (U.S.N.W.R., 1974).

In response to these growing constraints as well as to the downward filtering of innovative supermall architectural features and milieus, a new trend toward smaller shopping centers is emerging. A return to the single central department store surrounded by a more modest number of lavishly designed small shops is occurring (Rouse calls this arrangement the "jewel box" design in its new Exton Square center 30 miles west of Philadelphia), and malls entirely lacking large stores are being planned.

Tastefully designed smaller centers are often built around specialized themes, and with shrinking tributary areas it is likely that these kinds of facilities in the future will appeal and strongly cater to specific suburban socioeconomic and interest groups.

That the outer city has fully matured as the nation's retail pacesetter is now seen in the current attempts of central cities to emulate suburban successes. Large regional mall-type facilities have recently been opened or are under construction in both outer neighborhoods (Queens Center in New York) and downtown CBDs (Water Tower Place in Chicago, Market Street East in Philadelphia, and Broadway Plaza in Los Angeles), and smaller specialized centers are making inroads as well. The new suburban sophistication of the 1970s is also expressed in countless other ways, from the Picasso sculpture in Schaumburg's neighbor Rolling Meadows to the attitude expressed by a spokesman for New York's fashionable Lord and Taylor's on the opening of its own high prestige center of 25 stores adjacent to the superregional Garden State Plaza in northern New Jersey: "we certainly don't consider ourselves the Main Street of suburbia—we're its Fifth Avenue" (Morris, 1969, p. 9).

The Intrametropolitan Deconcentration of Employment

The deconcentration of intraurban employment, a steady trend since the interwar period (Figure 5), has also greatly accelerated since 1960. The dimensions of recent shifts in the suburban/central city share of metropolitan jobs are recorded in census data in Table 3 (columns 1-2). Detailed investigations of individual SMSAs reveal that city job losses in the 1960s alone surpassed those of the preceding 60 years (Hughes, 1974, p. 8). In the 1970s employment deconcentration within the metropolis has intensified further, and in 1973 the nation's suburbs pulled ahead of the central cities in total number of jobs. Accurate information on employment dispersal is difficult to obtain since the federal Bureau of Labor Statistics classifies metropolitan workers by place of residence rather than employment; moreover, sampling methods and data quality vary considerably from one metropolis to another. Among the 15 largest SMSAs listed in Table 3 post-1970 job estimates could be obtained only for New York and Philadelphia, and both confirm the persistence of a strong suburban trend. Suburban New York's share of regional employment rose from 35.9 percent in 1970 to 47.2 percent in 1974; over the same time period, suburban Philadelphia increased its SMSA job proportion from 51.8 to 54.3 percent.

The truly staggering city/suburb employment shift of more than 11 percent for metropolitan New York in just four years is underscored in recent reports in *The New York Times* (Sterne, 1974; Kihss, 1975), which are based on a reliable regional job monitoring system: (1) New York City's job losses of 1970–1972 wiped out all gains made during the previous decade; (2) in the 1972–1974 period substantial acceleration of job losses occurred in every occupational category except government and services; (3) from mid-1973 to mid-1974 the central city lost 41,000 jobs while the suburbs gained 35,000; and (4) the city's employment loss for the first nine months of 1975 was just under 200,000 jobs. Almost certainly, New York City's employment situation has been weakened further by its fiscal emergency which began in 1975. Even without this latest setback, the New York Regional Plan Association had already predicted that the city could not expect to capture more than 400,000 of the anticipated 2.4 million new jobs in the New York region between 1970 and 1985 (Cassidy, 1972, p. 22).

Because of growing suburban dominance in American metropolitan employment activity the lingering view of a dominant central city with dependent suburbs must be discarded. With a majority of metropolitan residents now working in the outer city, the notion of "bedroom suburbia" has become obsolete. Journey to work patterns reflect this and have shifted decisively since 1960; for example, in the 15 largest SMSAs the number of workers who both live and work in the suburbs has increased by at least three million (about 50 percent) and the number of reverse commuters has doubled to just under ten percent of the total work trips in these regions (Rosenthal, 1974b).

Whereas evidence signalling the emergence of the suburbs as the leading zone of intraurban employment is irrefutable, there is less agreement about the forces underlying this latest episode of job deconcentration. On one hand, many observers (especially in the popular press) claim that simultaneous city losses and suburban gains are the result of a simple decentralization process in which central city jobs merely relocate to the outer city. On the other, more cautious students of the urban scene insist that what appears in the raw data to be a simple outward drift of employment is actually a response to a more complex amalgam of noncomplementary push and pull forces whereby rapid absolute central city job losses happen to coincide with the vigorous expansion of new jobs in the suburbs. There can be no argument about suburban dominance of *new* employment activity—75 to 90 percent of the metropolitan jobs created since 1960 have been concentrated in the outer SMSA ring—but more research is needed to pin down how the overall dispersal mechanism operates.

A key to the controversy is that, given the ongoing

urbanization of the suburbs, there has been a pronounced erosion in metropolitan centrality as a locational attribute of the central city. This has affected different types of employment activity in different ways: while manufacturing has been quickest to respond to the new suburbanization forces, there are growing indications that tertiary, quaternary, and quinary office-based activities are beginning to respond similarly. These trends are consistent with the two remaining dimensions in Berry's interpretation (1973b, pp. 48-56; see page 13 above) of contemporary urbanization: *progressive intrametropolitan time-space convergence* and the *maturation of the postindustrial economy*. Let us focus on these dimensions by considering in turn the spatial dynamics of current manufacturing and office employment growth in the outer city.

The Suburbanization of Manufacturing Since 1960

Suburbanization of manufacturing was a trend underway before the turn of the century. Centrifugal forces in and around downtown (congestion, the lack of space, spiralling land values) combined with peripheral centripetal impulses (cheap and abundant land, low taxes, and good railroad access) to induce many manufacturers—particularly those engaged in the large-scale and mass production of standardized industrial goods—to decentralize their facilities outward along axial suburban rail corridors. However, the great majority of manufacturing operations requiring steady contact with local buyers and other firms, as well as smaller plants whose marketing and industrial functions were spatially inseparable, remained in or near center city until well into the 1960s; even the growing presence of the motor truck did not break this pattern until certain technological advances were achieved.

Industrial Location in the Contemporary Metropolis

These post-1960 breakthroughs involved the completion of the intraurban expressway system and the long-delayed attainment of scale economies in local trucking operations. Completing the freeway network made it possible to assemble goods at any number of points equally accessible to the rest of the metropolis, and newly economical short distance trucking helped neutralize the transportation cost differential between inner city and suburb. With the near equalization of these costs across much of the metropolis, intraurban goods movement via truck became as efficient as interregional freight transport. And by eliminating the locational pull of central city water and rail terminals, most of the remaining urbanization economies of downtown were quickly nullified.[16]

As metropolitan centrality advantages disappeared and as industrial location costs between the central city and suburban sites accessible to the regional freeway system approached equality, spatial constraints on city-based factories evaporated. Urban manufacturers responded to their newfound locational freedom by sharply increasing their activity in highly regarded suburban areas since the mid-sixties (see columns 5-6 in Table 3); concomitantly, central city investments have been reduced greatly, particularly in the old urban cores of the northeastern Manufacturing Belt where aging and often obsolescent inner city industrial facilities predominated. Putting these significant changes in intraurban economic geography into proper historical perspective, Berry and Cohen (1973, p. 454) conclude:

> The concentrated industrial metropolis *only* developed because proximity meant lower transportation and communication costs for those interdependent specialists who had to interact with each other frequently or intensively and could only do so on a face-to-face basis. But shortened distances also meant higher densities and costs of congestion, high rent, loss of privacy, and the like. As soon as technological change permitted, the metropolis was transformed to minimize these negative externalities.

As the metropolis is transforming into an all but frictionless area vis-a-vis goods movement, transportation costs no longer shape the spatial structure of its manufacturing activity. Thus intrametropolitan situation is increasingly irrelevant as a plant location variable, for industrial entrepreneurs are free to move to the "best" urban site they can find. Noneconomic factors come to the fore in such locational decision-making, and the perceived advantages of suburban sites are accentuated for just about every kind of industrial operation. Overriding these noncost-related forces today is the prestige factor in suburban industrial location, which is fast becoming central to an understanding of the contemporary spatial organization of urban manufacturing.

Prestige Considerations in Locational Decision-Making

The importance of status and corporate image in the functioning of today's industrial firms cannot be understated since manufacturers, like the general public, are highly susceptible to the latest social trends. In the last few years it has become highly fashionable to locate in booming new suburban areas, which are promoted enthusiastically by industrial realtors as style-setting centers containing the most exciting new metropolitan opportunities. Companies now spend lavishly to be in fashion, and the overwhelming concentration of these investments outside the central city confirms that entrepreneurs widely share this glamorous perception of the outer city. As but one example of this kind of

---

[16] Underscoring this trend is the ongoing decentralization of truck terminals to expressway-oriented suburban nodes; see Berry et al. (1976a, p. 27) for an account of these shifts in metropolitan Chicago, the nation's leading trucking center.

spatial behavior, Sternlieb cites the case of a Boston firm which forsook downtown site costs of $1.25 per square foot in order to relocate to a higher status suburban location where equivalent space sold for $4.75 (*U.S.N.W.R.*, 1971, p. 42).

Thus firms increasingly avoid low status areas such as the blighted inner city, much of the urban waterfront, and even the older suburban rail corridors whereas they covet prestigious outlying locations. Until recently high amenity residential suburbs were most prized for several obvious reasons, not the least of which was the chief executive's desire to minimize his personal commuting time; however, at the present time this type of location decision is being challenged vigorously (and with rising success) by local "no growth" advocates as well as by opponents of the exclusionary housing practices of wealthy municipalities. Much more important has been the gravitation of suburban industry to freeway corridors, not only for their superior accessibility but also for their priceless visibility, advertising, and image enhancement opportunities.[17] Practically every suburban expressway in the nation is lined with prominently displayed modern plants where site amenities (at least on the side facing the freeway) are given greater weight in facility design than production-related needs. Lately, industrial plants have indicated a stronger preference for expressway nodes, particularly those possessing the most glamorous suburban addresses in the proximity of superregional shopping malls.

Industrial Parks in the Outer City

Most accommodating for the lion's share of all but the largest manufacturing facilities in these vicinities are industrial parks (Mayer, 1964; Hartshorn, 1973), which in many ways are microcosms of the full range of locational advantages in the outer city of the 1970s. These organized industrial districts were first established in suburban Chicago at the turn of the century and gradually spread to other metropolitan areas through the efforts of railroads, which stood to profit doubly as both landlord and exclusive transport supplier at peripheral trackside locations. It was the postwar shift to freeways, however, which led to the rapid proliferation of the industrial park, and of the more than 2500 such facilities now in operation nearly 2000 have been developed since 1960.

Besides the traditional space and cost benefits of suburban location, contemporary industrial parks offer their tenants a number of special advantages. Foremost among them are their self-contained agglomeration economies arising from the proximal location of ultra-modern automated, horizontally arranged plants, which permit ready material and information linkages among firms. Sharing a large common site minimizes the costs of utilities, waste removal, and other public services, and makes possible more favorable leasing, financing, insurance, and local tax arrangements. The usually excellent accessibility of industrial parks, combined with the reinforced drawing power of their multiple employment opportunities, makes them especially atttractive to the increasingly diversified and skilled resident suburban labor force. Moreover, the satisfaction of working in these surroundings reduces labor turnover and in many suburbs the mere announcement of plans to construct such a new facility unleashes a deluge of job applications to the developer and his prospective tenants.

Above all, the industrial park powerfully emphasizes the prestige factor for its tenants by presenting a positive collective public image. Stylish park names as well as highly visible and glamorous main road addresses are deliberately sought. Attractive and even imaginative architecture and landscaping enhance the site. Compared to central city facilities, space is used lavishly in buildings, parking lots, and loading areas. The industrial parks provide a complete array of supporting services for tenants, among them private police and fire protection, building maintenance, executive clubs, employee cafeterias, and even recreational facilities.[18] Comprehensive site and situation planning stresses maximum unity with the surrounding environment as well as harmonious integration within the local community. Nuisance activities and obnoxious land uses are excluded, and the typical mix of companies consists of small and moderate sized (though scale of operations is increasing in the newest parks) light manufacturing, material fabrication, wholesale, and warehousing firms. Indeed, the efficiency of industrial parks is so advanced that a current trend toward specialized theme parks appears to be intensifying. Among the latter are: "fly-in" parks around airports such as suburban Chicago's O'Hare; research and development or science complexes like the Stanford (California) and Research Triangle (North Carolina) Industrial Parks, usually located near major universities; clusters of government facilities as in the Virginia and Maryland suburbs of Washington, D.C.; and the ubiquitous suburban office park (to be discussed later).

Suburban Industrial Growth Trends

The growing locational affinity of suburban manufacturers for each other as well as for certain activity nodes is a significant trend in the emerging

---

[17] A spectacular example is the 1976 decision by Volkswagen to locate its American assembly plant in New Stanton, Pennsylvania; this site in the outer suburbs of Pittsburgh, at the intersection of I-70 and the Pennsylvania Turnpike, is one of the most important expressway junctions in the Northeast. (VW's second choice was a similar location in suburban Cleveland.)

[18] This is epitomized in the new Tam O'Shanter Industrial Fairways park north of Chicago, built around nine holes of a former championship golf course (Berry *et al.*, 1976a, p. 38).

economic geography of the outer city. To some extent this mutual spatial gravitation is a long-standing phenomenon involving the suburban expression of classical external economies of localization, as seen in such older outlying clusters as the electronics industry west of Boston, steel fabrication around the Fairless Steel complex northeast of Philadelphia, and aircraft manufacturing in outer Los Angeles and on Long Island. By the early 1970s the critical mass of intrametropolitan manufacturing activity had become so firmly entrenched in the suburbs that many industries were establishing themselves in the outer city simply because so many others had found it profitable to do so. Moreover, today's industries tend to locate as closely as possible to established suburban facilities and business concentrations. Increasingly, a move by one firm will trigger similar location decisions by others: like people, industry will not locate just anywhere in the metropolis but will select sites accessible to the same services and labor force demanded by competitors (Schaeffer and Sclar, 1975, p. 59).

The emergence of suburbia as the leading zone of manufacturing necessitates a reinterpretation of the classical decentralization models, which view the outer urban ring merely as a reception area for companies emigrating from the central city. Wood (1974) has effectively attacked this core-dominated interpretation; by focusing instead on the metropolitan fringe, suburbia is quickly identified as a major zone of industrial expansion in its own right in which *self-generated* growth has been primarily responsible for its current preeminence. Given the recent suburbanization of entire industrial complexes and their supporting business facilities, the outer ring now functions as the dominant "incubator" location for new manufacturing firms. Moreover, as existing companies expand they usually seek to minimize the distance of new investment, and the resulting local dispersion of branch plants provides the other major internal source of industrial growth in the suburbs. External contributions also swell the suburban total, both from in-migrating central city firms (though to a much lesser extent than heretofore attributed) as well as from the branch facilities of extraregional national corporations whose locational strategies no longer require orientation to the metropolitan core.

We need to test this alternative explanation of urban manufacturing development further. Although data on industrial firm relocations are difficult to obtain, the limited information currently available indicates only modest numbers of direct city-to-suburb shifts. James and Hughes (1973) found that in heavily suburbanized New Jersey local outlying establishment growth (complemented by plant demise in adjacent central cities) dominated the process of manufacturing employment change, thus reemphasizing that understanding the spatial behavior of today's suburban firms is becoming increasingly independent of the scenarios predicted by traditional urban decentralization models.

Current Trends in the Location of Suburban Office Activity

Many of the same processes contributing to the prestige-related deconcentration of manufacturing are also working to reshape the intraurban distribution of office-based employment. After modest postwar beginnings, suburbanization of the office industry has accelerated since the mid-1960s. Pioneering sales offices of manufacturers were followed by large routine-operation insurance and other companies; they in turn were pursued by a myriad of smaller computer, research, and other service firms. In the next stage, regional offices of large national companies arrived, followed closely by a steadily rising number of major corporate headquarters. Finally, the dispersal of supposedly exclusively downtown-bound elitist office functions began (Manners, 1974, pp. 100-101). This suburban trend has intensified as the nation now completes its transition to a postindustrial economy dominated by information and communication-intensive activities. Thus the collection, processing, and distribution of information is becoming the key to today's wealth and power in a society where tertiary, quaternary, and quinary workers now account for about 75 percent of the labor force (Abler, 1974, p. 8).

Neutralization of the City-Suburb Differential in Office Location Advantages

The information-transactional office industry was traditionally located in the CBD, which possessed classical spatial advantages of metropolitan centrality as well as the benefits of face-to-face contact with other businessmen and immediate access to the ancillary services of outside specialists. As we have observed, however, the superior accessibility of downtown no longer obtains. More importantly, the once exclusive economic advantages of the CBD are being undercut by the changing needs of the industry which can be satisfied at newer outlying business centers. The result has been a rise in intrametropolitan locational independence, with many offices, like manufacturing plants, now free to concentrate at amenity- and prestige-rich sites in the outer city.

Economic factors governing office location—available space, labor, and ease of communication—certainly do not inhibit the current suburban trend. Land cost and space availability in the suburbs are frequently more favorable than in the CBD since a campus-style office complex costs only about one half of its equivalent square footage in a downtown skyscraper. However, this is a relatively unimportant cost differential because rent and local taxes amount to less than ten percent of total office expenditures (Manners, 1974, p. 98); the dominant cost component (80-90 percent) in running an office involves labor. Given the continuing dispersal of the metropolitan population and its overwhelming preference for commuting by automobile, the outer city now holds a commanding advantage in labor access. By locating at convenient highway sites with space for ample free parking, suburban offices easily attract workers and executives, and usually record much lower rates of employee turnover and absenteeism than those for counterpart CBD firms. A 1974 report by the Planning Commission of Long Island's Suffolk County documents the typically rapid growth of office employment in the outer city since 1970: half the county's office buildings have been constructed since 1970; the number of office jobs has doubled since 1965; and the potential office labor force residing locally has also doubled since the late sixties and will continue to expand rapidly as the New York City CBD no longer offers a net salary differential high enough to induce workers to commute to Manhattan.

Despite warnings that offices would not be able to function properly at a distance from the downtown business community, the overwhelming number of firms now operating in suburbia report no problems in maintaining interoffice communication. Although it is true that chance suburban meetings are fewer and that nearly every face-to-face transaction must be planned, it often requires no more time to drive to a conference in the outer city than it does to walk or take a cab to one in the CBD. New suburban business networks themselves have adapted with surprising speed, often by successfully combining professional dealings with luncheon meetings, or with informal contacts at cocktail parties and barbecues (Sommer, 1975, p. 141). The radial expressway system which, ironically, was designed to preserve the dominance of the postwar central city has actually helped accomplish the opposite with its peak-hour traffic jams that now make mid-day travel to the city infinitely more convenient (Schaeffer and Sclar, 1975, p. 54; Davis and Hartshorn, 1973). For those suburban office firms which must maintain continuous contact with downtown, telephones have proven quite adequate; moreover, the success and proliferation of such new telecommunication devices as picture phones, two-way cable TV, rapid facsimile, and computerized information transmission networks can only allow the further substitution of intraurban communication for individual travel and loosen ties to the CBD for a greater number of office activities (Harkness, 1973). Finally, suburban office location also means much easier highway access to other places, especially airports; this advantage is almost universally cited by executives of companies whose activities require frequent out-of-town trips.

CBD-bound ancillary activities have also begun to deconcentrate with the rapid emergence of the office industry in the suburbs. Whereas a few years ago suburbanizing firms often had to perform functions usually contracted to outside specialists, many suburban office concentrations today contain a full range of legal, tax, accountant, direct mail, public relations, advertising, management consultant, and countless other supporting business services. In a survey of these activities in the suburbs of southwestern Connecticut, Darnton (1974) found that they consisted of small-scale firms and were run by single independent businessmen who sought locations in small commercial buildings close to the office complexes of larger companies. Most specialized in rapid high quality service abetted by the availability of a large and skilled local labor pool. One highly pleased businessman informed Darnton that only the preceding day he had received his first order from Manhattan!

Changing Locational Decision-Making in the Metropolitan Office Industry

With intraurban space, labor, and communication advantages no longer heavily favoring the CBD, the spatial organization of the metropolitan office industry, like manufacturing before it, is increasingly responding to noneconomic locational forces (see Meyer, 1976). Because of the smaller size and decision-making structure of most office firms, management perception becomes the key location variable. Many critics of recent office moves from the central city have charged that personal convenience of the chief executive is the strongest motivation: by moving the company close to home the boss can minimize his own commuting. Although there may be some limited truth to this contention, given the current growth of office activity in high income residential suburbs, a far more serious charge claims that management prejudice has governed the relocation decision process. New York City's former economic development administrator, D. Kenneth Patton, bluntly contended recently that the changing ethnic composition of Manhattan's labor force has prompted corporate moves in order to preserve what he called "social distance":

> The executive decision-maker lives in a homogenized community. Increasingly his employees in the city are from communities very different in class and ethnicity.... The decision-maker can't relate to the city kid, that kid doesn't look the same to him. It's an older generation in charge trying to reestablish a setting that seems to be more comfortable, more the old way (Masotti and Hadden, 1974, p. 84).

This subjective line of reasoning, unsupported by any available evidence, is often espoused by emotional defenders of the central city who deliberately ignore the prevailing suburban spatial trend affecting all forms of economic activity. A more balanced view of ongoing intrametropolitan office deconcentration vis-a-vis executive perception shows that once again the overriding force is the prestige factor of today's highly fashionable suburbs.

Reinforcing this positive suburban perception is the growing negative attitude of many executives toward the CBD. This outlook varies according to city age and the strength of tradition with respect to downtown as an office center. The age and background of the executive himself also affects the firm's commitment to the CBD and there is no denying that the emerging generation of younger executives is far more likely to be of suburban rather than city origin. Young company officers are more likely to prefer less formal business environments, often because they have had first-hand junior executive experience with self-selected suburban office firms. Many corporations in the last few years have found it much easier to recruit and keep young executive talent at newer suburban facilities. On the other hand, many CBD companies are encountering resistance in attracting good young people who, in ever greater numbers, say they do not need the cultural amenities of downtown, the frustration of commuting there every day and immersion in what many perceive to be an increasingly tension-ridden central city business life. Moreover, the image and prestige level of many major cities has now reached a new low. In New York City, the latest financial emergency occurs at a time when the already staggering cost of doing business there is sharply rising. It is important to emphasize, however, that the suburbanization of the office industry would have occurred despite this latest setback. Union Carbide, which announced in early 1976 that it would move its headquarters staff of 3,500 from Manhattan to Danbury, Connecticut, succinctly summed up the prevailing attitude that corporations must above all else continue to be able to attract young talent:

> While we recognize that New York City does have many advantages, the long-term quality-of-life needs of our headquarters employees were the overriding factors in arriving at this conclusion (Sterne, 1976).

The Suburbanization of Corporate Headquarters

Although many believe that medium-size production-oriented offices and those performing routine operations such as computer billing could more readily disperse whereas large- and small-scale firms engaged in consumer-oriented and nonroutine office functions could not, the ongoing intrametropolitan deconcentration of major corporate headquarters has signalled a new phase in the suburbanization of the office industry. Nowhere is this spatial behavioral trend more apparent than in the decentralization of traditionally downtown-bound internation corporation headquarters from Manhattan to New York's suburbs.

Although complete data are not readily available, the press has kept its own count of the largest companies which have left Manhattan (Cassidy, 1972; Sterne, 1975). From 1969 to 1974, suburban New York registered a spectacular increase of from five to 50 corporate headquarters listed in *Fortune's* annual directory of the nation's 500 largest industrial firms; at the same time, New York City's share of these home offices has dwindled from 140 in the mid-1960s to just over 90 in 1976. Headquarters moves since the end of the sixties have been directed toward three suburban sectors. These areas and some of their most important new corporate citizens are: southwestern Connecticut, which is now close to passing Chicago as the country's second largest concentration of corporation offices (GE, GT&E, American Can, and Olin); Westchester County, bordering New York City on the north (General Foods, IBM, AMF, and Pepsico); and northern New Jersey (A&P, Allied Chemical, and Ingersoll-Rand). Even the Fantus Company, one of the largest location consulting firms in the country, has relocated itself just across the Hudson River to Englewood Cliffs, New Jersey (which also contains the home offices of Corn Products Corp., Volkswagen USA, Lipton, and Prentice-Hall) and, according to Fantus' chairman Leonard Yaseen, as many as 75 percent of the largest 200 remaining Manhattan corporations are considering seriously similar headquarter decentralization moves. Many, such as the Borden Company, have already done so unofficially by splitting up headquarters staffs: most of the company moves out while the chief executive's office remains behind with a residual work force of perhaps two or three dozen (Meyer, 1976, p. 272).

The growing appeal of the New York suburbs is by no means limited to Manhattan firms: also affected are corporate headquarters migrating into the region from elsewhere. When Xerox recently decided to move from Rochester to the New York area because of the latter's unparalleled national business and communications advantages, it also recognized that locating in New York City itself was no longer necessary (Abler, 1974, p. 56). The Xerox case is even more significant since that company encountered overwhelming local resistance in the community of its first choice, Greenwich, Connecticut, whose residents felt that accepting yet another gigantic office complex would forever destroy the town's character. Though defeated in Greenwich by the rising opposition of local "no growth" advocates, a movement now widespread in many heavily developed suburban areas, Xerox has since found a warmer reception for its new headquarters in nearby Stamford. Thus it is evident that despite difficulties, the suburban relocation process is still perceived by office firms as well worth the extra effort.

Although metropolitan New York has received the most publicity, the recent suburbanization of corporate head offices is a nationwide phenomenon.[19] No less than 135 of the "Fortune 500" companies (and 178 of the "second 500" ranked 501-1000) had headquarters in the suburbs in 1975, including three of the top nine. Compared to 1965 (47) and 1969 (56) totals for the top 500, this represents a truly significant increase. Although suburban New York did ac-

---

[19] Another corporate migration stream intensifying in the mid-1970s is the shift of headquarters away from the North and East to the so-called "Sunbelt" of the South and West (the latter in 1975 accounted for 117 of *Fortune's* top 500 companies) (Meyer, 1976). These moves are occurring at the macroscale for the same reasons they occur at the metropolitan level; in fact, "Sunbelt" headquarters sites very often are suburban or recently annexed outer central city locations (see Meyer's [1976, pp. 255-258, 262, 266] vignette of the Simmons Mattress Company's move to the Atlanta suburbs).

count for 104 of the home offices of *Fortune's* one thousand biggest 1975 corporations, an additional 207 of these headquarters were located in the suburbs of the next 20 largest SMSAs. Cassidy's (1972, p. 21) partial list, though now somewhat outdated, suggests the dimensions of suburban head office shifts around the country: Boston lost 75 large companies to its suburbs in 1970-71 and St. Louis 43 in 1970 alone; Los Angeles saw several major banks desert its CBD; and in Detroit, which recently lost S.S. Kresge, Bendix, Budd, and both of its daily newspaper offices to the suburbs, things are so depressing that former mayor Cavanaugh refers to "Detroit's sister cities—Nagasaki and Pompeii," and a sign at a business banquet not long ago read "Will the Last Company to Leave Detroit Please Turn Out the Lights."

Suburban Office Location Types

As the suburban office industry has matured in the last few years its internal distribution pattern has changed. Early postwar suburban offices, like manufacturing plants, were usually isolated and scattered widely among outlying sites offering good highway access. Although the high-amenity, single-company business campus concept was developed before 1950 (most notably by *Reader's Digest* in New York's Westchester suburb of Pleasantville), the innovation was slow to catch on until the late 1960s. A parallel trend, also pioneered shortly after the war but not widespread until two decades later, involved the growth of specialized centers containing concentrations of smaller offices.[20] By the early 1970s, however, both locational types came to dominate the suburban office scene. With the recent wave of major corporate headquarters decentralization, the business campus (now frequently dominated by high-rise structures) has been developed to a sophisticated and prestigious architectural level (Armstrong, 1972, pp. 158-163). Smaller centers have also proliferated rapidly since 1970 particularly in the form of office parks, the newest locational concept in the industry.

Suburban office parks (Hartshorn, 1973, pp. 42-43; Daniels, 1974, pp. 184-186) include many of the same attractions as industrial parks, especially prestigious addresses, self-contained concentrative economies, and easy access to other business centers. These kinds of facilities first developed as clusters of regional offices of national corporations (which explains the particular affinity of early office parks for sites near airports), but now appeal to the entire range of small to medium-size suburban firms. Office park development in recent years has therefore been considerable and is typified by suburban Atlanta which grew from one facility in 1964 to 40 office parks employing nearly 25,000 workers in 1974. The internal structure and range of supporting services in newer office parks emphasizes the ultimate in prestige and luxury: imaginative combinations of high- and low-rise buildings designed by famous architects; elegant restaurants and visitor reception areas; and such frills as swimming pools, tennis courts, saunas, and jogging and bike trails. The latest office park complexes are also growing larger in size (exceeding 3.5 million square feet) and are able to compete successfully for the most prized outer city locations. For example, the Oak Brook (Illinois) office park, which contains the head office of McDonalds, is located less than five miles from O'Hare Airport and two giant shopping malls, and adjoins a golf course as well as the Chicago area's largest motor hotel complex.

As office parks multiply and grow ever larger, they enhance the position of the suburbs as a site for complete white-collar business concentrations. Nearly every metropolis now contains at least one such high-prestige suburban office cluster, typified by Westchester's "Platinum Mile" of glamorous business complexes which line the central section of that county's major east-west expressway. As was the case with intraurban manufacturing activity, suburban moves by major office firms are now beginning to affect the location decisions of others. More than one corporation has recently shifted to the suburbs because its competitors have found it advantageous to do so. Although hard data and research are presently lacking, it is also likely that the sources of new suburban office activity are changing. In addition to companies leaving the CBD, it is highly probable that ongoing and near-future office growth in the suburbs will heavily involve in-migrating firms from outside the metropolis, self-generated expansion of existing outer city white-collar firms, and the indigenous birth of entirely new suburban office establishments.

The Changing Role of the CBD Office Complex

In spite of the prevailing suburban trend, a current interpretation of the intrametropolitan office industry must consider the still important role of the CBD. During the 1960s the centers of many large cities enjoyed an office job expansion and a building boom of unprecedented proportions. The continuing dominance of the downtown business community seemed all but assured. However, by the mid-1970s much of this optimism has subsided as it becomes apparent that the recent CBD revival trend has all but terminated in many metropolitan regions. Sunday newspapers today are no longer filled with glowing economic reports on downtown; one is far more likely to read about the glut of center city office space as hard-pressed commercial developers lower rents and raise fringe benefits in the fierce competition to attain tenancy thresholds in their new sky-

---

[20] One of the best known examples is Clayton, Missouri in the western suburbs of St. Louis, whose central regional location stimulated its early growth as a leading metropolitan office center (see Kersten and Ross, 1968).

scrapers. Increasingly, older CBD office buildings become the casualties as their former tenants take advantage of these bargains and flock to newer quarters, and vacancy rates rise at a time when energy and other operating costs sharply increase.

It is now obvious that builders overreacted to the heightened demand for downtown office space, a trend which peaked at the end of the sixties and has fallen steadily ever since. Unfortunately, the five-to ten-year lead time for planning new skyscrapers means that only now are developers beginning to respond to the changed market situation. Thus many already overbuilt CBDs are locked into commitments to continue building; for example, the Chicago Loop is supposed to add another 15 million square feet of office space by 1979. And desperate Manhattan with its deteriorating business environment is similarly committed, even though it has already built 56 million square feet of central office space in the seventies versus 46 million during the entire 1960s; as of late 1975 the CBD office vacancy rate was 12 percent and climbing, with more than 28 million square feet of such unoccupied space in new office towers alone (*Business Week,* 1975). To make matters worse, many of the CBD employment gains of the latter 1960s may have been short-lived. An early 1975 report (Kihss), which could be quite significant if it is the harbinger of an emerging national trend, revealed that New York City's brief economic recovery of 1973 was confined to its suburbs; new downtown office activity has turned out to be unexpectedly sensitive to recessions and has ceased growing.

The recent period of CBD office growth was based on supposedly unassailable centralized regional business community advantages. Yet there is now much evidence that traditionally downtown-bound office functions can operate successfully at many suburban locations. One of the most spatially conservative CBD office activities—banking—is a further case in point, and a recent study (Bies, 1974) sheds light on why so many banks have remained downtown and why they too may now be about to suburbanize. As the intraurban population disperses so do its banking habits, as people tend to use bank branches closest to home. Thus the pattern for metropolitan Washington, D.C. is typical, where the central city share of regional bank deposits deposits dropped from 73 to 50 percent in the 1960s and has probably declined at least another ten percent since 1970 (Grief, 1971, p. 45). However, the seemingly reluctant dispersion of branch offices in a majority of metropolitan areas is not at all a locational strategy aimed at preserving CBD banking dominance: in no less than 31 states in 1974 government regulatory agencies tightly restricted the number and distribution of branches, a policy dating back to the Depression belief that overbanking contributed to the number of bank failures. These regulations obviously favor the CBD, whose recent growth of bank activity may be more the result of suburban expansion constraints and central city consolidation through closings of high risk inner city branches than a resurgence of downtown economic dominance. Though little noticed, a reform movement is gathering momentum in the banking industry as government rules begin to be relaxed. Several states now permit affiliation arrangements between central city and suburban bank companies, and a few (most notably New York State) have recently permitted city banks to expand more widely into the suburbs and beyond. As these reforms continue to diffuse, they will almost certainly weaken the CBD's role in the metropolitan banking establishment. With the steady deconcentration of business, the comparative advantage of downtown as a commerical banking center will continue to decline. And the increasingly widespread use of automation, such as new methods of telephone and electronic fund transferring, will further lessen dependency on the CBD.

The eroding position of the CBD at the beginning of the last half of the 1970s is dramatically underscored by the Wall Street national financial community in lower Manhattan (Phalon, 1975; Narvaez, 1976). In response to ever increasing securities transfer taxes in New York City, more than a dozen major brokerage firms have begun to relocate their staffs to Jersey City and Hoboken just across the Hudson in tax-free New Jersey (5-10 minutes away from Wall Street by subway). A New Jersey state official claims this migration is now approaching the "floodgate" stage, and foresees the relocation of the entire securities industry by the mid-1980s. Even the New York Stock Exchange has threatened to pull out of the city as a bargaining ploy to hold down transfer tax increases, and, in undertaking a 1976-77 long-range expansion study, the American Stock Exchange has refused to rule out relocation to New Jersey or Connecticut as a possible future option.

Given the changing mix of push and pull forces now reshaping metropolitan office geography, what is the future outlook for the CBD vis-a-vis the suburbs? Despite the paucity of data and the lack of an appropriate office location theory, Manners (1974, esp. pp. 103-105) has recently offered a most thoughtful and balanced statement; he concludes that the central city in the future will attract only a steadily diminishing share of office activity whereas suburban office employment will increasingly become the norm. From the more up-to-date and wider ranging evidence considered above, the validity of this interpretation is fully supported here.

Manners builds his conclusion upon four interrelated and self-reinforcing factors. The first is that the major impact of private CBD reinvestment has already been felt. The building boom of the 1960s resulted from the desires of the private sector to preserve existing center city investments, and may well have amounted to the last defense of downtown against the persistent challenge of the economically burgeoning suburbs (which in many SMSAs added more new office space in the 60s than did the corresponding CBD). With established interests and remaining companies now housed in new structures, the future of this kind of CBD growth is expected to be limited. Second, suburban offices are proving viable for almost every type of urban-based office activity. Third, the changing origins of the outer city's office industry will enhance suburban growth opportunities. Self-generated development by expanding offices already located there combined with an increasingly important suburban role as a seedbed for newly formed white-collar companies will, in the immediate future, almost certainly trigger a new round of outlying office growth similar to the recent wave of manufacturing expansion in the suburbs. And fourth, changing intraurban accessibility relationships will continue to favor suburbia heavily. The shift to the freeway metropolis has greatly increased the number of attractive suburban sites and, as we noted, simultaneously has decreased the regional access advantage of downtown.

Even the arrival of new CBD-focused rapid transit systems in San Francisco, Washington, D.C., Atlanta, and a number of other large metropolitan areas in the coming decade will not alleviate center city's transporation dilemma (Lindsey, 1975a; also see Hamer and Hartshorn, 1974).Timing is all important; these recent commitments to improve public transportation follow the completion of the metropolitan expressway network, an irreversible reality and a powerful force in the growing strength of the suburban office industry (Manners, 1974, pp. 104-105). In fact, regional rapid transit innovations are likely to produce payoffs for the suburbs too, as Gannon and Dear's (1975) preliminary study of office development in suburban Philadelphia's Lindenwold Speedline corridor has shown.

Minicities and Suburban Spatial Oranization

Integration of the location trends shaping the suburban distribution of retailing, manufacturing, and the office industry shows a growing propensity for economic activities to gravitate toward each other. Pacesetting superregional shopping centers with their myriad social activities, complete attunement to the automobile, and regionwide drawing power via freeway, have become such focal points in the outer city. Their immediate vicinities assume an equally glamorous aura, and attract manufacturing and office employers whose current locational desires are fully satisfied at these prestigious sites highly accessible to labor and established suburban business facilities. The result has been the emergence of major multi-functional urban cores which are rapidly coming to dominate the economic geography of contemporary suburbia. Breckenfeld (1972, p. 80), among others, defines these suburban minicities as intricate and compact orchestrations of mixed land uses including shopping, employment, offices, wholesaling, entertainment, hotels, restaurants, and personal services such as medical facilities. Let us examine the minicity by first focusing on its internal organization, and then upon its increasingly powerful impact on the overall spatial structure of the suburbs.

Internal Organization of the Suburban Minicity

The internal structure of the minicity is typified by King of Prussia, Pennsylvania (Figure 10), a major suburban core adjacent to Valley Forge 20 miles northwest of downtown Philadelphia at the intersection of the Pennsylvania Turnpike, Schuylkill Expressway, and three other main suburban highways. Situated at the nucleus of the complex is King of Prussia Plaza, the Delaware Valley's second largest superregional shopping mall, which contains 1,300,000 square feet of selling space, five major department stores and 125 smaller shops. Distributed about the vicinity within a five minutes' drive of the mall are: dozens of highway-oriented retail facilities including two community shopping centers; one of the region's largest industrial park complexes (722 acres) containing the plants and warehouses of Western Electric, GM-Chevrolet, Borg Warner, Sears, Philco-Ford, three major pharmaceutical manufacturers, and 30 smaller companies; one of General Electric's major research and manufacturing facilities; a variety of office buildings and office parks, among them the home offices of Gino's (a leading Northeast fast food chain) and the American Baptist Convention; the Valley Forge Music Fair, a year-round theater offering top name entertainers weekly; five first-run cinemas; at least half a dozen fine restaurants; one of the area's best known cabarets; numerous superior quality high- and low-rise apartment complexes; and five large motor hotels with a total of more than 1500 rooms which in 1976 alone hosted 267 conventions.

Although the exact formula varies, the admixture of high order urban functions observed in the King of Prussia core (Figure 10) is quite representative of minicities which are materializing throughout the nation's suburbs. For reasons identical to those underlying the suburbanization of economic activity, cultural, leisure, and entertainment facilities are now also gravitating toward these new metropolitan nodes. In addition to live theater and first-run films, the suburbs have pioneered a new entertainment medium, the dinner theater (Rosenthal, 1974a). Culture is also flourishing in the outer city with the proliferation of centers such as Wolf Trap Farm Park for the Performing Arts (operated by the National Park Service), located in Vienna, Virginia just off suburban Washington's Capital Beltway and adjacent to the Tyson's Corner minicity (Hume, 1974). Recreational activities of every sort are heavily attracted to nodes in the outer city: professional sports is but one example, and in the 1970s the New England Patriots, Dallas Cowboys, California Angels, and Captial Bullets have been in the vanguard of a growing number of major league teams abandoning the inner city for luxurious new stadiums and arenas in the suburbs (Wallace, 1974). The glamor of minicities also attracts new hotels and high quality residential de-

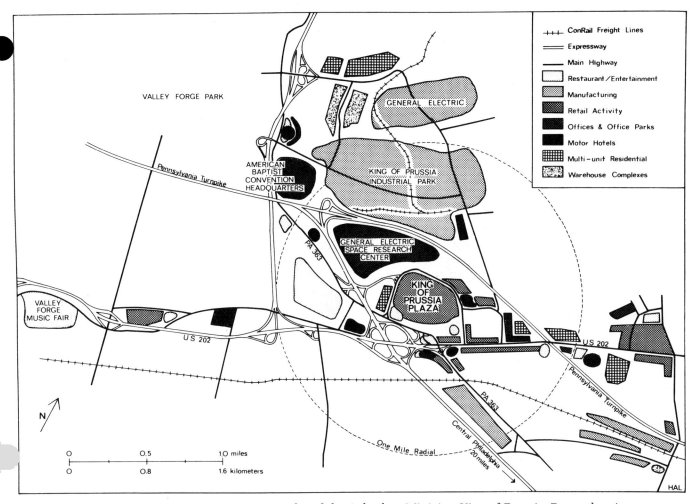

Figure 10. Internal Economic Geography of the Suburban Minicity: King of Prussia, Pennsylvania.

velopment. The suburbs have now become leading sites for both business conferences and larger conventions; typically, the Hyatt House chain in 1974 selected a suburban minicity (Cherry Hill, New Jersey) in which to build its first hotel in the Northeast. Increasingly, the most elegant new high- and low-rise condominium and apartment complexes are also lured toward suburban activity centers, which are coming to command some of the highest prices and rentals in the metropolis.

Although the minicity has helped revolutionize the geographical structure of heretofore centerless suburbia, a number of corollary spatial problems are encountered in all but a small handful of carefully planned cores. The King of Prussia map (Figure 10) clearly illustrates the central problem: a lack of internal cohesion among component activities. This intraminicity hodgepodge pattern results from the independent actions of developers and builders whose uncoordinated location decisions guarantee a piecemeal and haphazard accretion of uses as the land adjacent to the nuclear shopping mall is filled in. Thus what emerges is not a true multi-functional core but rather a loose cluster of isolated and specialized uni-functional subcenters, a development process Gruen (1973, pp. 90-91) documents for a number of suburban minicities. Internal mobility, then, is the major spatial shortcoming as short distance auto travel, usually among parking lots separated by less than a mile, is required in order to move from the site of one function to that of another. The internal minicity dispersion of activities and parking facilities also forces the dangerous mixing of slow-moving short distance and higher speed through traffic on interconnecting main roads as well as adding greatly to local highway congestion, the latter exacerbated by the growing size of individual enterprises which continue to cluster in and attract even more traffic to the expanding core.

Although a few voluntary attempts are being made toward alleviating these problems through better planning—most notably in comprehensively planned unit developments or "PUDs" such as Echelon in southern New Jersey where the developer (Rouse) owns and controls a wide zone of surrounding land in order to resist the disorderly encroachment of other activities near the central retail-employment core—the almost universal lack of stringent nonresidential land controls assures that most suburban minicities will remain inefficiently structured agglomerations. Though little will be done to improve the internal arrangement of existing suburban cores, rapidly rising land costs in such superior access locations should in the future foster tighter activity clustering and more intensive use of space. Accordingly, Douglass (1974) predicts that minicities will evolve into high-rise "omnicenters" characterized by more intensified vertical uses of space featuring multi-level complexes of mixed activities built over indoor parking facilities.

Minicities are most likely to develop around the most accessible suburban points where two expressways intersect. There are, however, numerous activity concentrations of smaller proportions which are appearing at less superior locations on the suburban highway network, and many may well become the minicities of tomorrow. These lesser multifunctional centers are often partially formed minicities in that one element, such as the superregional mall or industrial park complex, is missing; others may be incipient suburban cores whose activities have not yet reached a scale to qualify them for minicity status. Another emerging type of multi-purpose suburban center is associated with the localization of some special activity: airports in particular have lately assumed such a growth pole function.

Almost every major metropolis now possesses a suburban airport-expressway complex consisting of shopping centers, industrial parks, residential and office towers, and clusters of motor hotels. These complexes have enormous prestige value and may radiate outward for several miles along main airport approach routes. The area around O'Hare International Airport outside Chicago is one of the best examples (Berry and Cohen, 1973, pp. 446-447). Throughout the area, businessmen frequently use the prestigious "O'Hare" name to identify with the glamorous jet age image of "the world's busiest airport." Not surprisingly, fully one third of suburban Chicago's office space has been attracted to O'Hare's vicinity, and at least 75 percent of the 25,000 employees at Centex Industrial Park in neighboring Elk Grove Village reverse commute from the central city's blue-collar neighborhoods. And as a hotel-convention-entertainment center, the O'Hare area has become "Chicago's Second City" with nearly 50 hotels, 7500 guest rooms (early 1970s), and a year-round occupancy rate in excess of 90 percent.[21]

[21] The same locational affinity for suburban airport cores is also affecting the distribution of overseas-oriented office activity. For example, Coral Gables, Florida near suburban Miami's International Airport has become the major center for the Latin American headquarters of many U.S. corporations, among them Exxon, Dow Chemical, Texaco, Goodyear, and about 50 others (*Parade Magazine*, 1976).

Minicities, Beltways, and the Emerging Spatial Structure of the Outer City

Although individual minicities now serve as the foci of large segments of suburbia, at the metropolitan scale one observes that an increasingly unified system of minicities and lesser suburban activity concentrations is coming to dominate the spatial structuring of the entire outer city. This multi-nodal system is shaped primarily by the configuration of the interconnecting freeway network, and particularly by the circumferential expressway or beltway linking each of the various suburban sectors of the metropolis.

The circumferential superhighways were originally conceived as bypasses around major cities, but rapid development after World War II of the peripheries of these urban centers soon provided such arteries with a more important function: to serve the large new suburban population which had settled in its girdling corridor. The nation's first limited-access high speed circumferential, Massachusetts Route 128, constructed around Boston in the late 1940s and early 1950s, was an early response to the region's postwar suburbanization. Route 128 was built not to satisfy existing travel demands but rather to make the automobile the primary metropolitan transport mode to facilitate intersuburban trip-making (Schaeffer and Sclar, 1975, pp. 90-91). This highly successful expressway shaped the population growth of Boston's suburbs in the fifties. Also known as the "Electronics Highway," a name not really deserved since that dispersing industry was only attracted to the superhighway's general vicinity, Route 128 had a powerful appeal to many other employers and retailers who flocked to locate within the corridor.

The 1956 Federal Interstate Highway Act spurred the diffusion of the circumferential freeway. The intercity expressways mandated by this law required that central city bypass routes be built in most metropolitan areas, especially in the large conurbations of the northeastern seaboard Megalopolis, where the original bypass links constructed around major cities (e.g., Baltimore's Harbor Tunnel Thruway) were often later extended into complete beltways.

By the early seventies more than 80 beltways were in operation, and even in metropolises containing only partially circumferential freeways the attractions of these corridors promoted suburban economic activity. Although the peak access interchanges (where two or more expressways converge) were likeliest to spawn complete minicities, highly visible corridor segments lying between exits were also prized for their free advertising potential and are often lined solidly with eye-catching plants, office buildings, and apartment complexes.

The growing locational pull of such high status beltways as Atlanta's Perimeter and Houston's Loop will dominate the post-1975 suburbanization of people and activities. They also affect outer city facilities which predated the construction of beltways. Large

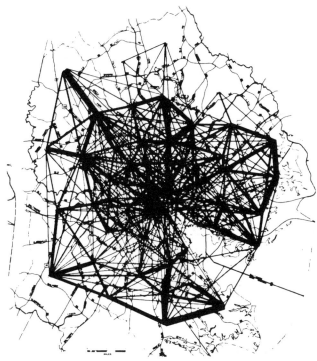

Figure 11. Forecasted 1980 Travel Desires Among Internal Districts of Metropolitan Baltimore. Reproduced by permission of the National Academy of Sciences.
Source: Avery, 1972, p. 14.

retail and employment centers often induced planners to route new freeways near them; their operations increasingly focus on the new opportunities created by rapid growth within recently opened circumferential corridors; and their own physical expansion stimulated by this suburban development is likely to be spatially attuned to the beltway, particularly the nucleating forces exerted by minicities. Hughes (1974, p. 4) captures the flavor of this ongoing movement:

> Vast arcs of economic activity have sprouted along newly-completed circumferential roadways, which are dotted with the physical monuments to the suburban success story. Regional shopping centers, office towers, and sprawling campus-style corporate headquarters represent the fullest flowering of the historic migration out of American cities. Huge numbers of Americans live, work, play, shop and dine within the physical confines of this freeway culture [as the suburbs emerge] as entities independent of the older central cities which they surround.

Thus we are now witnessing the rise of a continuous unitary curvilinear outer city whose circumferential freeway spine functions as both lifeline and main street of suburbia and is increasingly the key to understanding its overall spatial organization. The consequences of this trend for total intrametropolitan travel flows can be observed in Figure 11. This 1980 traffic pattern forecast for the Baltimore region, based on a projection of early 1970s flow data, shows the dominance of circumferential automobile travel focused on various suburban activity cores, with only seven percent of the traffic destined for the CBD (Ward and Paulhus, 1974, p. 25).

The travel flows predicted in Figure 11 may be conservative given the continuing remarkable development along suburban Baltimore's Beltway. Known locally as the "Golden Horseshoe," this corridor is capturing much of the productive activity in the metropolis. Several important suburban facilities were already located close to its path (e.g., Bethlehem Steel's vast Sparrows Point complex which employs more than 30,000 workers); and major employers such as the U.S. Social Security Administration (13,000 employees), which recently relocated from the central city to its new headquarters office complex adjacent to the Beltway in the western suburb of Woodlawn, continue to be attracted in rising numbers. Moreover, the Golden Horsehoe is unique in that it lies within the single political jurisdiction of suburban Baltimore County,[22] thus overcoming the development conflicts which frequently occur among municipalities.

One outcome of the centralization of political power in Baltimore County is that the county seat, Towson, not only retains its influence but has become the region's most important suburban minicity

---

[22] County governments in Maryland still retain considerable political power.

(only a handful of minicities have evolved from old suburban towns). Located at the apex of the Golden Horseshoe alongside the Beltway, Towson has attracted, apart from the usual high order retail, industrial, and office park clusters, most of Baltimore County's government buildings and such high-level services as a three-hospital medical complex. Towson also contains Maryland's largest women's college (Goucher) and a large state college (Towson State), with the latter's drawing power and growth significantly increased by regionwide Beltway access since the mid-1960s. The local skyline is now dominated by high rise structures like Hampton Plaza, whose builder has crisply summarized why developers continue to be so strongly attracted to suburban beltway nodes:

> This is the city. They're getting out of Baltimore ... I could see Mohammed wasn't going to the mountain anymore, so I said, "Let's build the mountain out here." That's what I bet on (Masotti and Hadden, 1974, p. 270).

The success of suburban Baltimore's circumferential expressway corridor has been equalled and surpassed in the adjoining suburbs of the District of Columbia to the southwest where the Capital Beltway has truly become the main street of metropolitan Washington. Although the nation's capital and its suburbs have sometimes been regarded as an atypical urban area with little to teach the rest of the United States, there are those who insist that it is now possible to view the District region as a metropolis "where the problems are basically the same as those in most others, but often more clearly defined" (Grier, 1971, p. 45). Since the Washington metropolis was one of the first to complete its suburban beltway and especially since it grew more rapidly in the 1960s than any of the other largest SMSAs, what is happening there may indeed be indicative of national trends.

Since 1960, nearly one million new residents have settled in the Capital Beltway corridor. A dozen regional malls as well as several other major suburban activity nuclei have sprung up at nearly every one of the 38 exits along the freeway's 66-mile length. New employment is burgeoning with the federal government playing a leading role in the economic development of the corridor. Nearly half the region's federal jobs have dispersed from the District of Columbia, with a sizeable proportion of them now located along the Beltway. This decentralization trend began prior to the construction of the Beltway, and many government facilities situated in or near the circumferential corridor enjoyed enhanced accessibility and rapid expansion with the arrival of the expressway. Among the myriad large headquarters and branch offices of federal agencies which are found in this suburban corridor are: HEW's Public Health Service, Commerce's Bureau of the Census, Defense's Department of the Navy, The National Agricultural Research Center, The Central Intelligence Agency, The Atomic Energy Commission, and The National Bureau of Standards; the last two facilities are located a short distance beyond the girdling corridor but draw most of their work force via the Beltway, and all except the Census Bureau grew to their present major size in the suburbs following construction of the circumferential expressway.[23]

As the huge office complexes of the federal government disperse to the Maryland and Virginia suburbs, they create an enormous impact on the communities to or from which they move. Since many employ thousands of modestly skilled workers who reside in Washington's inner city, the social consequences of the suburbanization of these facilities are generally negative. Despite the rising protest of the District's blacks and other disadvantaged groups about their greatly reduced access to these suburban jobs which are frequently relocated from central city neighborhoods, the federal government seems to be acting no differently from other employers who abandon the city with little regard for the problems of the labor force left behind.

Perhaps the most far-reaching impact of the Capital Beltway and its sister circumferential freeways is that they foster suburban self-sufficiency and independence. With multi-functional minicities offering the full array of urban goods and services and with driving times such that half the Beltway can be traversed in less time than it takes to travel from any point on it into downtown Washington, a steadily increasing number of suburban residents are avoiding the central city altogether.

Suburban Avoidance of the Central City and the Metropolitan Future

As scholarly interest in contemporary suburbanization and its consequences intensifies, the term *urbanization of the suburbs* itself is coming to mean "the growing economic, cultural and political independence of suburbia" from the central city which spawned it (Masotti, 1975, p. vii).[24]

A sampling of recent press reports (Rosenthal, 1974c; *U.S.N.W.R.*, 1972, and Karasik, 1973) reveals

---

[23] Private business activity is also growing very rapidly in the burgeoning Beltway corridor as the postindustrial economy matures and companies increasingly cluster around information-rich Washington, D.C. (Webber, 1968, p. 1096). Although major corporate headquarters have not yet been attracted to relocate to the Washington suburbs, the mid-1976 announcements that Mobil Oil Corporation was shifting its chief domestic operating division from Manhattan to Falls Church, Virginia and Time-Life Books from Manhattan to Alexandria, Virginia may be harbingers of things to come.

[24] As suburbs achieve freedom from reliance on the nearby central city, they will depend increasingly on other places, many of them distant, to which they are connected by a growing complex of road, airplane, cable, computer, and even satellite networks (Birch, 1975, p. 31). This shattering of intrametropolitan interdependency in the 1970s marks an important watershed in American urban history. A wholly new settlement geography is emerging, of which contemporary suburbia is an integral component (see Adams and Abler, 1976).

an emerging consensus of suburban perception of the central city: irrelevant. Everything the suburban resident requires now lies within easy automobile reach in the outer city, and when a rare good or service is not available a close suburban substitute is usually accepted in place of the undesirable trip to center city; not surprisingly, most suburbanites interviewed either could not remember their last visit downtown or recalled only a single trip there in connection with a special occasion. Scholarly investigations of this form of spatial avoidance behavior are lacking and urgently need to be undertaken. In fact, in the entire pre-1976 social science literature on suburbia only one published research report directly addresses this question: Zikmund's (1971) brief and now dated study of the frequency of downtown use by affluent and well-educated residents of one of Philadelphia's wealthiest suburban Main Line townships. He found that even in this hardly typical municipality, with its excellent commuter rail connection and strong traditional working, shopping, and cultural ties to center city Philadelphia, trends similar to those now reported in the popular media were observed: suburbanites, especially middle-class families, increasingly have no use for the central city, and what contact does occur is directly related to daily commuting to the CBD (which has been declining since 1960).

Detachment from the central city can be interpreted according to the demographic composition of today's suburban population. The postwar generation is to a large degree suburban-born without first-hand experience in true city living. Moreover, the lion's share of recent migration to the suburbs has come not from the adjacent central city but from largely suburban origins in other metropolitan areas (Birch, 1975). Thus,

> Most new suburbanites have no ties whatsoever to the old [central] city. It is not the hub of their cultural, economic, material, or social lives; it is not their previous home; it is *nothing* to them—just another place (not even a relatively large place) in their sprawling metropolitan home territory. What impact do arguments of moral responsibility or abstract dependency have for these people? Virtually none (Zikmund, 1975, p. 43)

The deepening schism between city and suburban ring is highly significant for the immediate future of the metropolis. Fava (1975, pp. 14-15) sees the suburbs as possessing a disproportionate share of those "who are 'better off,' highly participatory and influential" but whose attitude toward urban problems is increasingly one of "tolerant aloofness and noninvolvement," a posture which does not augur well for the selling of metropolitanism as the answer to the worsening plight of the nation's cities (see Raskin, 1975).

Given this suburban attitude, what, then, is to become of the central cities? The intrametropolitan deconcentration of the most vital population groups and a critical mass of economic activities cannot continue for much longer before we become a nation with no important cities (see Patterson, 1976). Though many urban planners and other enthusiastic proponents of city living insist that central cities are recoverable, trends shaping the metropolitan reality as the twentieth century ends would dictate otherwise. The big city is not yet dead, but its economic and cultural *raisons d'être* are disappearing. When one adds to this the declining municipal tax base, continuing residential disinvestment, and out-migration of middle and upper income groups, what does the former core city have left to offer?

The city is becoming a social dumping ground for the most disadvantaged segments of the metropolitan population. Thus the main crisis of the central city today is one of function, which according to Sternlieb (1971, pp. 17-18) has essentially become that of *sandbox:*

> A sandbox is a place where adults park their children in order to converse, play, or work with a minimum of interference. The adults, having found a distraction for the children, can get on with the serious things of life. There is some reward for the children in all this. The sandbox is given to them as their own turf. Occasionally, fresh sand or toys are put in ... with an implicit admonition that these things are furnished to minimize the level of noise and nuisance. If the occupants ... start bashing each other over the head, the adults will come running, ... calm things down, and then ... bring fresh sand and fresh toys, pat the occupants of the sandbox on the head, and disappear once again into their adult involvements and pursuits.

Government programs for the inner city, in particular, are seen as the height of sandboxism:

> ... money has been used to create a growing bureaucracy which is sustained by the plight of the poor, ... but which yields little in the way of loaves and fishes to the poor.... When old programs begin to lose their credibility or become unfashionable, they are given new names ... [they] have become forms of symbolic action. In their ritualistic aspects they are of particular value. They give psychic satisfaction to the patrons of the poor, convince outsiders—especially the media—that "something is being done," and indicate to the urban poor that some one up there really cares. In a word, these programs are placebos, and they often produce all the authentic, positive results which placebos can have in medical practice (Sternlieb, 1971, p. 18).

At best these failing programs are benign. At their worst they reinforce the unlivability of inner city neighborhoods by supplying economic incentives to create "social sinkholes," as amply demonstrated in a recent study of New York City's fire-decimated South Bronx where the urban decay process has all but run its course toward utter destruction (Meyer, 1975).

Although society seems to have opted for the sandbox approach to the problems of the central city, it is still not too late to develop strategies and implement public policies that can restore some of the economic and social functions of the old metropolitan core. However, as Sternlieb (1971, p. 21) reminds us,

> ... if we define the problems of the city as the gap between the reality of the cities as they exist today and a romanticized fantasy of cities as they used to be—as the economic center of the nation, as the font of civility and graciousness, as the source of everything that warms the hearts of social critics—then those problems are simply unsolvable ....

Therefore, in order to have a chance at success, programs designed to attack economic problems must, above all, clearly recognize the sharply reduced role of the central city in today's suburban-dominated multi-nodal metropolis.

Perhaps a time will come again when large cities will have a leading role to play in urban America. For the foreseeable future, however, Irving Kristol's (1974, p. 282) pronouncement is worth keeping in mind:

> ... we can say with fair certainty that we are moving toward an urban civilization without great cities—and that this movement is so without precedent that prophecies of doom or hopes of utopia are both premature.

BIBLIOGRAPHY

Since the literature on contemporary suburbia is both diverse and almost completely outside the discipline of geography, a brief bibliographical guide is provided here. Sources referred to are starred in the alphabetical listing below.

Good general introductions to the field are *City*, Fischer, Palen, Sobin (1971), Masotti and Hadden (1974), *Time*, and the *U.S. News and World Report* (1972). Anthologies containing original scholarly essays on suburbia are Masotti and Hadden (1973), Hawley and Rock, and Schwartz (1976b); useful readers containing reprints of earlier work are Downes, Haar (1972), Kramer, and Hughes (1974). Comprehensive works on aspects of suburbanization are Wirt *et al.* and Baker on political dimensions, and Thorns on sociological aspects. The only geographical volume to date is Johnson's (1974b) collection of essays which is focused away from the American experience for the most part; the special issue of *City* contains brief vignettes of the suburbs of some major metropolitan areas.

Jackson's (1973) penetrating but all too brief statement reviews the historical evolution of the suburbs. Warner (1962) treats late nineteenth-century suburbs; H. Douglass and Wilson cover early twentieth-century development. Holt, Tarr, and Schaeffer and Sclar deal with the historical linkage between suburbs and transportation technology.

General coverage of suburban social structure is found in Masotti (1975), Schwartz (1976b), Kaplan (1976a), Dobriner (1963), and Hall. Suttles (1975) and Michelson treat contemporary community forms; Gans' (1967) classic case study of Levittown is still a most fertile work. The masterful photographic essay by Owens (1973) documents daily life in middle-class California suburbs.

The economic organization of contemporary suburbia has yet to be studied in depth. Breckenfeld (1972) and Berry and Cohen discuss the restructuring of the metropolis. James and Hughes, and Wood focus on manufacturing change. Manners, Hartshorn, and Abler treat suburbanization of the office industry; Quante reviews the exodus of corporate headquarters from New York City.

In addition to the compilation below, other current bibliographies on the outer city are Masotti and Dennis, and various reading lists which accompany Masotti and Hadden (1973), Hawley and Rock, and Schwartz (1976b).

References and Further Reading

*Abler, R. F. (1974), *Employment Shifts and Transportation Policy: Changes in the Locations of Corporate Headquarters in Pennsylvania, 1950-1970*. Pennsylvania State University, Pennsylvania Transportation Institute.

Adams, J. S. (1969), "Directional Bias in Intra-Urban Migration," *Economic Geography*, 45:302-323.

_____ (1970), "Residential Structure of Midwestern Cities," *Annals of the Association of American Geographers*, 60:37-62.

_____ (ed.) (1976a), *Contemporary Metropolitan America: Twenty Geographical Vignettes*. Cambridge, Mass.: Ballinger Publishing Company, Association of American Geographers, Comparative Metropolitan Analysis Project.

_____ (ed.) (1976b), *Urban Policy-Making and Metropolitan Dynamics: A Comparative Geographical Analysis*. Cambridge, Mass.: Ballinger Publishing Company, Association of American Geographers, Comparative Metropolitan Analysis Project.

Adams, J. S. and R. F. Abler (1976), "National, State, and Local Policy Considerations," in R. F. Abler (ed.), *A Comparative Atlas of America's Great Cities: Twenty Metropolitan Regions*. Minneapolis: University of Minnesota Press, Chapter 49.

Anastasia, G. (1975), "Mt. Laurel: Responsibility vs. Reality—'Moral Victory' Won't Build Homes," *The Philadelphia Inquirer*, October 12, 1-B - 4-B.

Armstrong, R. B. (with B. Pushkarev, [ed.]) (1972), *The Office Industry: Patterns of Growth and Location*. Cambridge, Mass.: The MIT Press.

Avery, W. H. (1972), "Practical Requirements for Advanced Public Transportation Systems," *Highway Research Record*, 397:12-25.

Babcock, R. F. (1973), "Exclusionary Zoning: A Code Phrase for a Notable Legal Struggle," in L. H. Masotti and J. K. Hadden (eds.), *The Urbanization of the Suburbs*. Beverly Hills: Sage Publications, Urban Affairs Annual Reviews, 7:313-328.

*Baker, E. M. (ed.) (1975), "The Suburban Reshaping of American Politics," *Publius*, Winter, 5:1-144.

Bederman, S. H. and J. S. Adams (1974), "Job Accessibility and Underemployment," *Annals of the Association of American Geographers*, 64:378-386.

Bensman, J. and A. Vidich (1971, 1975), "The New Class System and Its Life Styles," in S. D. Feldman and G. W. Thielbar (eds.), *Life Styles: Diversity in American Society*, 2nd rev. ed. Boston: Little, Brown and Company, pp. 129-143.

Berger, B. M. (1960), *Working Class Suburb: A Study of Auto Workers in Suburbia*. Berkeley: University of California Press.

_____ (1965, 1971), "Suburbs, Subcultures, and Styles of Life," in B. M. Berger, *Looking for America: Essays on Youth, Suburbia, and Other American Obsessions*. Englewood Cliffs, N. J.: Prentice-Hall, Inc., pp. 165-187.

Bergman, E. M. (1974), *Eliminating Exclusionary Zoning: Reconciling Workplace and Residence in Suburban Areas*. Cambridge, Mass.: Ballinger Publishing Company.

Berry, B. J. L. (1973a), "Contemporary Urbanization Processes," in F. E. Horton (ed.), *Geographical Perspectives and Urban Problems*. Washington, D.C.: National Academy of Sciences, pp. 94-107.

_____ (1973b), *The Human Consequences of Urbanisation*. New York: St. Martin's Press.

——————— (1975), "Short-Term Housing Cycles in a Dualistic Metropolis," in G. Gappert and H. M. Rose (eds.), *The Social Economy of Cities*. Beverly Hills: Sage Publications, Urban Affairs Annual Reviews, 9:165-182.

*Berry, B. J. L. and Y. S. Cohen (1973), "Decentralization of Commerce and Industry: The Restructuring of Metropolitan America," in L. H. Masotti and J. K. Hadden (eds.), *The Urbanization of the Suburbs*. Beverly Hills: Sage Publications, Urban Affairs Annual Reviews, 7:431-455.

Berry, B. J. L., I. Cutler, E. H. Draine, Y. Kiang, T. R. Tocalis, and P. de Vise (1976a), *Chicago: Transformations of an Urban System*. Cambridge, Mass.: Ballinger Publishing Company, Association of American Geographers, Comparative Metropolitan Analysis Project.

Berry, B. J. L., C. A. Goodwin, R. W. Lake, and K. B. Smith (1976b), "Attitudes Toward Integration: The Role of Status in Community Response to Racial Change," in B. Schwartz (ed.), *The Changing Face of the Suburbs*. Chicago: The University of Chicago Press, pp. 221-264.

Bies, S. S. (1974), "The Suburbanization of Banking Services." Paper presented at the Regional Science Association Meeting.

Birch, D. L. (1970), *The Economic Future of City and Suburb*. New York: Committee for Economic Development, CED Supplementary Paper No. 30.

——————— (1975), "From Suburb to Urban Place," *The Annals of the American Academy of Political and Social Science*, 422:25-35.

Bittan, D. (1972), "Levitt or Leave It." *Philadelphia Magazine*, September, 79-85, 190-195.

Blumberg, L. and M. Lalli (1966), "Little Ghettoes: A Study of Negroes in the Suburbs," *Phylon*, 27:117-131.

Blumenthal, R. (1968, 1974), "The Suburban Poor," in L. H. Masotti and J. K. Hadden (eds.), *Suburbia in Transition*. New York: New Viewpoints for *The New York Times*, pp. 212-216.

Boal, F. W. (1968), "Technology and Urban Form," *Journal of Geography*, 67:229-236.

Bradford, C. P. and L. S. Rubinowitz (1975), "The Urban-Suburban Investment-Disinvestment Process: Consequences for Older Neighborhoods," *Annals of the American Academy of Political and Social Sciences*, 422:77-86.

* Breckenfeld, G. (1972), " 'Downtown' Has Fled to the Suburbs," *Fortune*, October, 80-87, 156, 158, 162.

——————— (1976), "Is the One-Family House Becoming a Fossil? Far From It," *Fortune*, April, 84-89, 164-165.

Brodsky, H. (1973), "Land Development and the Expanding City," *Annals of the Association of American Geographers*, 63:159-166.

Browning, C. E. (ed.) (1974), *Population and Urbanized Area Growth in Megalopolis, 1950-1970*. University of North Carolina at Chapel Hill, Department of Geography, Studies in Geography No. 7.

Bruce-Biggs, B. (1974), "Gasoline Prices and the Suburban Way of Life," *The Public Interest*, Fall, 37:131-136.

Buder, S. (1967), *Pullman: An Experiment in Industrial Order and Community Planning, 1880-1930*. New York: Oxford University Press.

Business Week (1975), "New York City's Real Estate Mismatch," October 13, 108, 110, 113.

Buttimer, A. (1972), "Community," in M. Stewart (ed.), *The City: Problems of Planning–Selected Readings*. Baltimore: Penguin Books, Inc., pp. 195-216.

Caldwell, E. (1972, 1974), "The Problems of a Black Suburb," in L. H. Masotti and J. K. Hadden (eds.), *Suburbia in Transition*. New York: New Viewpoints for *The New York Times*, pp. 78-81.

Caldwell, W. A. (ed.) (1973), *How to Save Urban America: Key Issues Confronting Cities and Suburbs*. New York: Signet Books.

Campbell, C. C. (1976), *New Towns: Another Way to Live*. Reston, Va.: Reston Publishing Company, Inc.

Carver, H. (1965), *Cities in the Suburbs*. Toronto: University of Toronto Press.

Cassidy, R. (1972), "Moving to the Suburbs," *The New Republic*, January 22, 20-23.

Chinitz, B. (ed.) (1964), *City and Suburb: The Economics of Metropolitan Growth*. Englewood Cliffs, N. J.: Prentice-Hall, Inc.

Christian, C. M. (1975), "Emerging Patterns of Industrial Activity Within Large Metropolitan Areas and Their Impact on the Central City Work Force," in G. Gappert and H. M. Rose (eds.), *The Social Economy of Cities*. Beverly Hills: Sage Publications, Urban Affairs Annual Reviews, 9:213-246.

**City*, Magazine of Urban Life and Environment* (1971), "The Suburbs: Frontier of the 70s," January-February.

Clark, S. D. (1966), *The Suburban Society*. Toronto: University of Toronto Press.

Clawson, M. (1971), *Suburban Land Conversion in the United States*. Baltimore: Johns Hopkins University Press.

Clay, G. (1973), *Close-Up: How to Read the American City*. New York: Praeger Publishers.

Cohen, Y. S. (1972), *Diffusion of an Innovation in an Urban System: The Spread of Planned Regional Shopping Centers in the United States, 1949-1968*. Chicago: University of Chicago, Department of Geography, Research Paper No. 140.

Cohen, Y. S. and B. J. L. Berry (1975), *Spatial Components of Manufacturing Change*. University of Chicago, Department of Georgraphy, Research Paper No. 172.

Colby, C. C. (1933), "Centrifugal and Centripetal Forces in Urban Geography," *Annals of the Association of American Geographers*, 23:1-20.

Connell, J. (1974), "The Metropolitan Village: Spatial and Social Processes in Discontinuous Suburbs," in J. H. Johnson (ed.), *Suburban Growth: Geographical Processes at the Edge of the Western City*. London: John Wiley & Sons, Ltd., pp. 77-100.

Connolly, H. X. (1973), "Black Movement Into the Suburbs: Suburbs Doubling Their Black Populations During the 1960s," *Urban Affairs Quarterly*, 9:91-111.

Cottingham, P. H. (1975), "Black Income and Metropolitan Residential Dispersion," *Urban Affairs Quarterly*, 10:273-296.

Cox, K. R. (1973), *Conflict, Power and Politics in the City: A Geographic View*. New York: McGraw-Hill Book Company.

Crouch, W. W. and B. Dinerman (1968), "Decentralization in Megalopolis," in M. D. Speizman (ed.), *Urban America in the Twentieth Century*. New York: Thomas Y. Crowell Co., pp. 194-200.

Cutler, I. (1973), *Chicago: Metropolis of the Mid-Continent*. Chicago: The Geographic Society of Chicago.

Daniels, P. W. (1974), "New Offices in the Suburbs," in J. H. Johnson (ed.), *Suburban Growth: Geographical Processes at the Edge of the Western City*. London:

John Wiley & Sons, Ltd., pp. 177-200.

Danielson, M. N. (1972), "Differentiation, Segregation, and Political Fragmentation in the American Metropolis," in A. E. K. Nash (ed.), *Governance and Population: The Governmental Implications of Population Change*. Washington, D.C.: Commission on Population Growth and the American Future, Research Reports Vol. 4, pp. 143-176.

Darnton, J. (1971, 1974), "The Service Industries Follow the Corporations," in L. H. Masotti and J. K. Hadden (eds.), *Suburbia in Transition*. New York: New Viewpoints for *The New York Times*, pp. 90-94.

Davidoff L., P. Davidoff, and N. N. Gold (1971, 1974), "The Suburbs Have to Open Their Gates," in L. H. Masotti and J. K. Hadden (eds.), *Suburbia in Transition*. New York: New Viewpoints for *The New York Times*, pp. 134-150.

Davidoff, P., L. Davidoff, and N. Gold (1970), "Suburban Action: Advocate Planning for an Open Society," *Journal of the American Institute of Planners*, 36:12-21.

Davis, S. and T. A. Hartshorn (1973), "How Does Your City Grow? The Changing Pattern of Activity Location in the Atlanta Metropolitan Area," *Atlanta Economic Review*, July-August, 4-13.

Dawson, J. A. (1974), "The Suburbanization of Retail Activity," in J. H. Johnson (ed.), *Suburban Growth: Geographical Processes at the Edge of the Western City*. London: John Wiley & Sons, Ltd., pp. 155-175.

Delaney, P. (1971, 1974a), "Negroes Find Few Tangible Gains," in L. H. Masotti and J. K. Hadden (eds.), *Suburbia in Transition*. New York: New Viewpoints for *The New York Times*, pp. 278-282.

_____ (1974b), "Dayton Suburbs Tackle Problems of 'Fair Share' Housing," *The New York Times*, November 17, 67.

Deskins, D. R., Jr. (1972), "Race, Residence, and Workplace in Detroit, 1880 to 1965," *Economic Geography*, 48:79-94.

Dingemans, D. J. (1975a), "The Townhouse in the Suburbs: Changing Housetypes and Social Space." Paper presented to the 71st annual meeting of the Association of American Geographers. Mimeographed.

_____ (1975b), "The Urbanization of Suburbia: The Renaissance of the Row House," *Landscape*, 20:20-31.

*Dobriner, W. M. (1963), *Class in Suburbia*. Englewood Cliffs, N. J.: Prentice-Hall, Inc.

_____ (ed.) (1958), *The Suburban Community*. New York: G. P. Putnam's Sons.

Donaldson, S. (1969), *The Suburban Myth*. New York: Columbia University Press.

*Douglass, H. P. (1925), *The Suburban Trend*. New York: The Century Company.

Douglass, L. (1974), "Tomorrow: Omnicenters on the Landscape?," *Harvard Business Review*, March-April, 8, 12.

*Downes, B. T. (ed.) (1971), *Cities and Suburbs: Selected Readings in Local Politics and Public Policy*. Belmont, Cal.: Wadsworth Publishing Company, Inc.

Downs, A. (1973), *Opening Up The Suburbs: An Urban Strategy for America*. New Haven: Yale University Press.

_____ (1974), "Squeezing Spread City," *The New York Times Magazine*, March 17, 38-40, 42, 44, 46-47.

Duncan, J. S. (1973), "Landscape Taste as a Symbol of Group Identity: A Westchester County Village," *Geographical Review*, 63:334-355.

Eaton, L. K. (1963-64), "The American Suburb: Dream and Nightmare," *Landscape*, Winter, 13:12-16.

Edel, M., J. R. Harris, and J. Rothenberg (1975), "Urban Concentration and Deconcentration," in A. H. Hawley and V. P. Rock (eds.), *Metropolitan America in Contemporary Perspective*. New York: Halsted Press, Division of John Wiley & Sons, and Sage Publications, Inc., pp. 123-156.

Elazar, D. J. (1966, 1972), "Are We A Nation of Cities?," in C. M. Haar (ed.), *The End of Innocence: A Suburban Reader*. Glenview, Ill.: Scott, Foresman and Company, pp. 8-13.

_____ (1975), "Suburbanization: Reviving the Town on the Metropolitan Frontier," *Publius*, Winter, 5:53-80.

Epps, R. W. (1969), "Suburban Jobs and Black Workers," *Business Review*, Federal Reserve Bank of Philadelphia, October, 3-13.

Epstein, B. J. (1967), "The Trading Function," in J. Gottmann and R. A. Harper (eds.), *Metropolis on the Move: Geographers Look at Urban Sprawl*. New York: John Wiley & Sons, Inc., pp. 93-101.

Erber, E. (1970), "Jobs Go Where the Poor Can't," *Manpower*, U.S. Department of Labor, September, 2-7.

Ernst, R. T. (1976), "Growth, Development, and Isolation of an All-Black City: Kinloch, Missouri," in R. T. Ernst and L. Hugg (eds.), *Black America: Geographic Perspectives*. Garden City, N. Y.: Doubleday-Anchor Books, pp. 368-388.

Fagin, H. (1958), "Problems of Planning in the Suburbs," in W. M. Dobriner (ed.), *The Suburban Community*. New York: G. P. Putnam's Sons, pp. 362-371.

Farley, R. (1964), "Suburban Persistence," *American Sociological Review*, 29:38-47.

_____ (1970), "The Changing Distribution of Negroes Within Metropolitan Areas: The Emergence of Black Suburbs," *American Journal of Sociology*, 75:512-529.

Farrell, W. E. (1974), "Suburb Weighs Curb on Blacks In Bid to Spur Racial Integration," *The New York Times*, February 10, 46.

_____ (1976), "Impact of Court's Ruling on Low-Income Housing Is Seen Far Off," *The New York Times*, April 26, 42.

Fava, S. F. (1975), "Beyond Suburbia," *Annals of the American Academy of Political and Social Science*, 422:10-24.

Feldman, S. D. and G. W. Thielbar (eds.) (1975), *Life Styles: Diversity in American Society*, 2nd rev. ed. Boston: Little, Brown and Company.

Fellows, L. (1975), "Hartford Battles Suburbs for Federal Aid," *The New York Times*, November 17, 33, 51.

_____ (1976), "Hartford Blocks Aid for Suburbs," *The New York Times*, January 29, 1, 58.

*Fischer, C. S. (1976), "The Suburban Experience," in *The Urban Experience*. New York: Harcourt Brace Jovanovich, Inc., Chapter 9, pp. 204-233.

Foley, D. L. (1973, 1975), "Institutional and Contextual Factors Affecting the Housing Choice of Minority Residents," in S. Gale and E. G. Moore (eds.), *The Manipulated City: Perspectives on Spatial Structure and Social Issues in Urban America*. Chicago: Maaroufa Press, Inc., pp. 168-181.

Fosburgh, L. (1975), "Coast City Upheld on Broad Growth Curbs," *The New York Times*, August 17.

Fried, J. P. (1971, 1972), *Housing Crisis U.S.A.* Baltimore: Penguin Books.

Frieden, B. J. (1972), "Blacks in Suburbia: The Myth of Better Opportunities," in L. Wingo (series ed.), *Minority Perspectives.* Baltimore: Johns Hopkins University Press, for Resources for the Future, Inc., The Governance of Metropolitan Regions No. 2, pp. 31-49.

Gallion, A. B. and S. Eisner (1975), *The Urban Pattern: City Planning and Design,* 3rd rev. ed. New York: D. Van Nostrand Company.

Gannon, C. A. and M. J. Dear (1975), "Rapid Transit and Office Development," *Traffic Quarterly,* 29:223-242.

Gans, H. J. (1962), "Urbanism and Suburbanism as Ways of Life: A Re-evaluation of Definitions," in A. Rose (ed.), *Human Behavior and Social Processes.* Boston: Houghton Mifflin Co., pp. 625-648.

*—————— (1967), *The Levittowners: Ways of Life and Politics in a New Suburban Community.* New York: Vintage Books.

—————— (1968, 1974), "The White Exodus to Suburbia Steps Up," in L. H. Masotti and J. K. Hadden (eds.), *Suburbia in Transition.* New York: New Viewpoints for *The New York Times,* pp. 46-61.

Glantz, F. B. and N. J. Delaney (1973), "Changes in Nonwhite Residential Patterns in Large Metropolitan Areas, 1960 and 1970," *New England Economic Review,* Federal Reserve Bank of Boston, March-April, 2-13.

Glazer, N. (1974), "On 'Opening Up' the Suburbs," *The Public Interest,* Fall, 37:89-111.

Glenn, N. D. (1973), "Suburbanization in the United States Since World War II," in L. H. Masotti and J. K. Hadden (eds.), *The Urbanization of the Suburbs.* Beverly Hills: Sage Publications, Urban Affairs Annual Reviews, 7:51-78.

Goering, J. M. and E. M. Kalachek (1973), "Public Transportation and Black Unemployment," *Transaction-Society,* July-August, 39-42.

Goheen, P. G. (1974), "Interpreting the American City: Some Historical Perspectives," *Geographical Review,* 64:362-384.

Gold, N. N. (1972), "The Mismatch of Jobs and Low-Income People in Metropolitan Areas and Its Implications for the Central-City Poor," in S. M. Mazie (ed.), *Population, Distribution, and Policy.* Washington, D.C.: Commission on Population Growth and the American Future, Research Reports Vol. 5, pp. 441-486.

Gordon, M. (1971a), "Los Angeles," *City, Magazine of Urban Life and Environment,* January-February, 23-26.

—————— (1971b), *Sick Cities.* New York: The Macmillan Company.

Grier, G. (1971), "Washington: A Beltway is 'Creating New Patterns Which Increase the Independence of the Suburbs from Their Parent',*" City, Magazine of Urban Life and Environment,* January-February, 45-49.

Gruen, N. J. and C. Gruen (1972), *Low and Moderate Income Housing in the Suburbs: An Analysis for the Dayton, Ohio Region.* New York: Praeger Publishers.

Gruen, V. (1973), *Centers for the Urban Environment.* New York: Van Nostrand Reinhold Co.

Guterbock, T. M. (1976), "The Push Hypothesis: Minority Presence, Crime, and Urban Deconcentration," in B. Schwartz (ed.), *The Changing Face of the Suburbs.* Chicago: The University of Chicago Press, pp. 137-161.

*Haar, C. M. (ed.) (1972), *The End of Innocence: A Suburban Reader.* Glenview, Ill.: Scott, Foresman and Company.

—————— (ed.) (1974), *Suburban Problems: The President's Task Force, Final Report.* Cambridge, Mass.: Ballinger Publishing Company.

Haar, C. M. and D. S. Iatridis (1974), *Housing the Poor in Suburbia: Public Policy at the Grass Roots.* Cambridge, Mass.: Ballinger Publishing Company.

Hadden, J. K. and J. J. Barton (1973), "An Image That Will Not Die: Thoughts on the History of Anti-Urban Ideology," in L. H. Masotti and J. K. Hadden (eds.), *The Urbanization of the Suburbs.* Beverly Hills: Sage Publications, Urban Affairs Annual Reviews, 7:79-119.

Hahn, H. (1973), "Ethnic Minorities: Politics and the Family in Suburbia," in L. H. Masotti and J. K. Hadden (eds.), *The Urbanization of the Suburbs.* Beverly Hills, Sage Publications, Urban Affairs Annual Reviews, 7:185-209.

*Hall, P. (1968), "The Urban Culture and the Suburban Culture," in R. Eells and C. Walton (eds.), *Man in the City of the Future: A Symposium of Urban Philosophers.* London: Collier-Macmillan Ltd., pp. 99-145.

Hamer, A. M. (1973), *Industrial Exodus From Central City: Public Policy and the Comparative Costs of Location.* Lexington, Mass.: D. C. Heath and Company.

Hamer, A. and T. A. Hartshorn (1974), "Planning Massive Accessibility for Central Atlanta: A Study of Misleading Projections," *High Speed Ground Transportation Journal,* 8:291-302.

Harkness, R. C. (1973), "Communication Innovations, Urban Form and Travel Demand: Some Hypotheses and a Bibliography," *Transportation,* 2:153-193.

Harris, C. D. (1943), "Suburbs," *American Journal of Sociology,* 49:1-13.

Harris, C. D. and E. L. Ullman (1945), "The Nature of Cities," *Annals of the American Academy of Political and Social Science,* 242:7-17.

Hart, J. F. (1975), *The Look of the Land.* Englewood Cliffs, N. J.: Prentice-Hall, Inc.

*Hartshorn, T. A. (1973), "Industrial/Office Parks: A New Look for the City," *Journal of Geography,* 72:33-45.

Harvey, D. (1972), *Society, The City and the Space-Economy of Urbanism.* Washington, D.C.: Association of American Geographers, Commission on College Geography, Resource Paper No. 18.

*Hawley, A. H. and V. P. Rock (eds.) (1975), *Metropolitan America in Contemporary Perspective.* New York: Halsted Press, Division of John Wiley & Sons, and Sage Publications, Inc.

*Holt, G. E. (1972), "The Changing Perception of Urban Pathology: An Essay on the Development of Mass Transit in the United States," in K. T. Jackson and S. K. Schultz (eds.), *Cities in American History.* New York: Alfred A. Knopf, pp. 324-343.

Hoover, E. M. (1968), "The Evolving Form and Organization of the Metropolis," in H. S. Perloff and L. F. Wingo, Jr. (eds.), *Issues in Urban Economics.* Baltimore: Johns Hopkins Press, for Resources for the Future, Inc., pp. 237-284.

Hoover, E. M. and R. Vernon (1959), *Anatomy of a Metropolis: The Changing Distribution of People and Jobs Within the New York Metropolitan Region.* Cambridge, Mass.: Harvard University Press.

Horvath, R. J. (1974), "Machine Space," *Geographical Review,* 64:167-188.

Hughes, J. W. (1975), "Dilemmas of Suburbanization and

Growth Controls," *Annals of the American Academy of Political and Social Science,* 422:61-76.

* _____ (ed.) (1974), *Suburbanization Dynamics and the Future of the City.* New Brunswick, N.J.: Rutgers University, Center for Urban Policy Research.

Hughes, J. W. and F. J. James (1974), "Suburbanization Dynamics and the Transportation Dilemma," in J. W. Hughes (ed.), *Suburbanization Dynamics and the Future of the City.* New Brunswick, N.J.: Rutgers University, Center for Urban Policy Research, pp. 19-42.

Hume, P. (1974), "Acres for the Arts," *Opera News,* June, 22-25.

Jackson, K. T. (1972), "Metropolitan Government Versus Suburban Autonomy: Politics on the Crabgrass Frontier," in K. T. Jackson and S. K. Schultz (eds.), *Cities in American History.* New York: Alfred A. Knopf, pp. 442-462.

* _____ (1973), "The Crabgrass Frontier: 150 Years of Suburban Growth in America," in R. A. Mohl and J. F. Richardson (eds.), *The Urban Experience: Themes in American History.* Belmont, Cal.: Wadsworth Publishing Company, Inc., pp. 196-221.

_____ (1975), "Urban Deconcentration in the Nineteenth Century: A Statistical Inquiry," in L. F. Schnore (ed.), *The New Urban History: Quantitative Explorations by American Historians.* Princeton: Princeton University Press, pp. 110-142.

* James, F. J., Jr. and J. W. Hughes (1973), "The Process of Employment Location Change: An Empirical Analysis," *Land Economics,* 49:404-413.

Jensen, H. (1976), "Defeat for Builders, California Cities Can Limit Growth," *Sacramento Bee,* March 7.

Johnson, J. H. (1974a), "Geographical Processes at the Edge of the City," in J. H. Johnson (ed.), *Suburban Growth: Geographical Processes at the Edge of the Western City.* London: John Wiley & Sons, Ltd., pp. 1-16.

* _____ (ed.) (1974b), *Suburban Growth: Geographical Processes at the Edge of the Western City.* London: John Wiley & Sons, Ltd.

Johnston, R. J. (1968), "Railways, Urban Growth and Central Place Patterns: An Example From South-East Melbourne," *Tijdschrift Voor Economische en Sociale Geografie,* 59:33-41.

Kain, J. F. (1968), "The Distribution and Movement of Jobs and Industry," in J. Q. Wilson (ed.), *The Metropolitan Enigma: Inquiries Into the Nature and Dimensions of America's "Urban Crisis".* Cambridge, Mass.: Harvard University Press, pp. 1-43.

Kaplan, S. (1971), "The Balkanization of Suburbia," *Harper's Magazine,* October, 72-74.

* _____ (1976a), *The Dream Deferred: People, Politics, and Planning in Suburbia.* New York: The Seabury Press.

_____ (1976b), " 'THEM'—Blacks in Suburbia," *New York Affairs,* Winter, 3:20-41.

Karasik, E. (1973), "Philadelphia No Longer Is 'Hub of World' to Suburbanites: Bedroom Communities Grow to Mini-Cities," *Philadelphia Inquirer,* February 9, 1-A - 8-A.

Kasarda, J. D. (1972), "The Impact of Suburban Population Growth on Central City Service Functions," *American Journal of Sociology,* 77:1111-1124.

_____ (1976), "The Changing Occupational Structure of the American Metropolis: Apropos the Urban Problem," in B. Schwartz (ed.), *The Changing Face of the Suburbs.* Chicago: The University of Chicago Press, pp. 113-136.

Kasarda, J. D. and G. V. Redfearn (1975), "Differential Patterns of City and Suburban Growth in the United States," *Journal of Urban History,* 2:43-66.

Kersten, E. W., Jr. and D. R. Ross (1968), "Clayton: A New Metropolitan Focus in the St. Louis Area," *Annals of the Association of American Geographers,* 58:637-649.

Kihss, P. (1975), "Migration From the Metropolitan Area Viewed by Planning Group as Threat," *The New York Times,* January 30.

King, S. S. (1971, 1974), "Suburban 'Downtowns': The Shopping Centers," in L. H. Masotti and J. K. Hadden (eds.), *Suburbia in Transition.* New York: New Viewpoints for *The New York Times,* pp. 101-104.

*Kramer, J. (ed.) (1972), *North American Suburbs: Politics, Diversity, and Change.* Berkeley: The Glendessary Press, Inc.

Kristol, I. (1972, 1974), "America's Future Urbanization," in J. W. Hughes (ed.), *Suburbanization Dynamics and the Future of the City.* New Brunswick, N.J.: Rutgers University, Center for Urban Policy Research, pp. 271-282.

Kron, J. (1973), "An Infiltrator's Guide To the Main Line," *Philadelphia Magazine,* June, 114-117, 168-171.

Lieberson, S. (1962), "Suburbs and Ethnic Residential Patterns," *American Journal of Sociology,* 67:673-681.

Lindsey, R. (1975a), "Mass Transit, Little Mass," *The New York Times Magazine,* October 19, 17, 82-88.

_____ (1975b), "Experts Say Housing Programs Fail to Open Suburbs to the Poor," *The New York Times,* November 11.

Lineberry, R. L. (1975), "Suburbia and the Metropolitan Turf," *Annals of the American Academy of Political and Social Science,* 422: 1-9.

Louis, A. M. (1975), "The Worst American City," *Harper's Magazine,* January, 67-71.

*Manners, G. (1974), "The Office in Metropolis: An Opportunity for Shaping Metropolitan America," *Economic Geography,* 50:93-110.

Masotti, L. H. (1973), "Prologue: Suburbia Reconsidered—Myth and Counter-Myth," in L. H. Masotti and J. K. Hadden (eds.), *The Urbanization of the Suburbs.* Beverly Hills: Sage Publications, Urban Affairs Annual Reviews, 7:15-22.

* Masotti, L. H. (guest ed.) (1975), "The Suburban Seventies," *Annals of the American Academy of Political and Social Science,* 422:vii-151.

*Masotti, L. H. and D. E. Dennis (1974), *Suburbs, Suburbia, and Suburbanization: A Bibliography,* 2nd rev. ed. Monticello, Ill.: Council of Planning Librarians, Exchange Bibliography Nos. 524-525.

*Masotti, L. H. and J. K. Hadden (eds.) (1973), *The Urbanization of the Suburbs.* Beverly Hills: Sage Publications, Urban Affairs Annual Reviews, Vol. 7.

* _____ (eds.) (1974), *Suburbia in Transition.* New York: New Viewpoints for *The New York Times.*

Masters, S. H. (1975), *Black-White Income Differentials: Empirical Studies and Policy Implications.* New York: Academic Press, Research on Poverty Monograph Series.

Mayer, H. M. (1964), "Centex Industrial Park: An Organized Industrial District," in R. S. Thoman and D. J. Patton (eds.), *Focus on Geographic Activity: A Collec-*

tion of Original Studies. New York: McGraw-Hill Book Company, pp. 135-145.

─────────── (1969), *The Spatial Expression of Urban Growth.* Washington, D.C.: Association of American Geographers, Commission on College Geography, Resource Paper No. 7.

McKay, R. V. (1973), "Commuting Patterns of Inner-City Residents," *Monthly Labor Review,* November, 43-48.

McKee, D. L. and G. H. Smith (1972), "Environmental Diseconomies in Suburban Expansion," *The American Journal of Economics and Sociology,* 31:181-188.

Meyer, H. E. (1975), "How Government Helped Ruin the South Bronx," *Fortune,* November, 140-146, 150, 154.

─────────── (1976), "Why Corporations Are on the Move," *Fortune,* May, 252-258, 262, 266, 270, 272.

*Michelson, W. H. (1976), *Man and His Urban Environment: A Sociological Approach,* 2nd rev. ed. Reading, Mass.: Addison-Wesley Publishing Company.

Mills, D. (1973), "Suburban and Exurban Growth," in *The Spread of Cities.* Milton Keynes, U.K.: The Open University Press, Social Sciences Second Level Course, Urban Development Units 23-25, pp. 51-102.

Mills, E. S. (1970), "Urban Density Functions," *Urban Studies,* 7:5-20.

Morris, J. H. (1969), " 'Meet Me at the Mall'—Big Shopping Centers Are Becoming the Focus of Life in the Suburbs," *Wall Street Journal,* February 20, 1, 9.

Muller, P. O. (1974), "Urbanization in Suburban Delaware Valley: The Recent Growth of the Philadelphia Urbanized Area," in C. E. Browning (ed.), *Population and Urbanized Area Growth in Megalopolis, 1950-1970.* Chapel Hill, N.C.: University of North Carolina, Department of Geography, Studies in Geography No. 7, pp. 71-83.

─────────── (1975), "Social Transportation Geography," in C. Board, R. J. Chorley, P. Haggett, and D. R. Stoddart (eds.), *Progress in Geography: International Reviews of Current Research.* New York: St. Martin's Press, Vol. 8, pp. 208-230.

Narvaez, A. A. (1976), "Jersey Says It's Getting 5 More Wall St. Firms," *The New York Times,* February 5.

National Research Council (1975), *Toward an Understanding of Metropolitan America.* San Francisco: Canfield Press, for the National Academy of Sciences.

Nelson, H. J. (1959), "The Spread of An Artificial Landscape Over Southern California," *Annals of the Association of American Geographers,* Supplement, 49:80-100.

Newsday (1973), "The Real Suburbia," *LI Magazine,* April 29, 7-29.

Newsweek (1971), "The Battle of the Suburbs," November 15, 61-64, 69-70.

Neutze, M. (1968), *The Suburban Apartment Boom: Case Study of a Land Use Problem.* Baltimore: Johns Hopkins Press, for Resources for the Future, Inc.

Norwood, L. K. and E. A. T. Barth (1966, 1972), "Urban Desegregation: Negro Pioneers and Their White Neighbors," in C. M. Haar (ed.), *The End of Innocence: A Suburban Reader.* Glenview, Ill.: Scott, Foresman and Company, pp. 118-123.

Oser, A. S. (1976), "Supreme Court Ruling in Chicago Case Is Likely to Have Only a Limited Effect," *The New York Times,* April 22.

Outtz, J. H. (1974), "Area Real Estate Advertising Practices Improving but Some 'Questionable' Wordings Remain," *Metropolitan Bulletin: Agenda for the 70s,* Washington, D.C.: Center for Metropolitan Studies, August, 4.

*Owens, B. (1973), *Suburbia.* San Francisco: Straight Arrow Books.

─────────── (1975), *Our Kind of People: American Groups and Rituals.* San Francisco: Straight Arrow Books.

*Palen, J. J. (1975), "Life-Styles: The Suburbs," *The Urban World.* New York: McGraw-Hill Book Company, Chapter 7, pp. 147-175.

Parade Magazine (1976), "Coral Gables Rising," Intelligence Report Section, February 8.

Patterson, J. (1976), "The Prospect of A Nation With No Important Cities," *Business Week,* February 2, 66, 69.

Pendleton, W. W. (1973), "Blacks in Suburbs," in L. H. Masotti and J. K. Hadden (eds.), *The Urbanization of the Suburbs.* Beverly Hills: Sage Publications, Urban Affairs Annual Reviews, 7:171-184.

Phalon, R. (1975), "Will Jersey City Replace Wall St.?," *The New York Times,* October 12, Section 3, 1, 4.

Pinkerton, J. R. (1969), "City-Suburban Residential Pattern by Social Class: A Review of the Literature," *Urban Affairs Quarterly,* 4:499-519.

Platt, R. H. (1976), *Land Use Control: Interface of Law and Geography.* Washington, D.C.: Association of American Geographers, Resource Paper No. 75-1.

Population Bulletin (1972), "Suburban Growth—A Case Study," *Population Bulletin,* February.

Pred, A. R. (1964), "The Intrametropolitan Location of American Manufacturing," *Annals of the Association of American Geographers,* 54:165-180.

*Quante, W. (1976), *The Exodus of Corporate Headquarters from New York City.* New York: Praeger Publishers.

Rabin, Y. (1973), "Highways As a Barrier to Equal Access," *Annals of the American Academy of Political and Social Science,* 407:63-77.

Rainwater, L. (1966), "Fear and the House-as-Haven in the Lower Class," *Journal of the American Institute of Planners,* January, 32:23-30.

─────────── (1972, 1975), "Post-1984 America," in H. I. Safa and G. Levitas (eds.), *Social Problems in Corporate America.* New York: Harper & Row, Publishers, pp. 371-378.

Raskin, A. H. (1975), "New York City's Neighbors Want No Part of Its Troubles," *The New York Times,* June 8, Section 4, 1.

Rose, H. M. (1969), *Social Processes in the City: Race and Urban Residential Choice.* Washington, D.C.: Association of American Geographers, Commission on College Geography, Resource Paper No. 6.

─────────── (1972), "The All Black Town: Suburban Prototype or Rural Slum?," in H. Hahn (ed.), *People and Politics in Urban Society.* Beverly Hills: Sage Publications, Urban Affairs Annual Reviews, 6:397-431.

Rosenthal, J. (1972, 1974a), "The Cultural Boom in the Suburbs," in L. H. Masotti and J. K. Hadden (eds.), *Suburbia in Transition.* New York: New Viewpoints for *The New York Times,* pp. 105-108.

─────────── (1972, 1974b), "The Rapid Growth of Suburban Employment," in L. H. Masotti and J. K. Hadden (eds.), *Suburbia in Transition.* New York: New Viewpoints for *The New York Times,* pp. 95-100.

─────────── (1971, 1974c), "Toward Suburban Independence," in L. H. Masotti and J. K. Hadden (eds.),

Suburbia in Transition. New York: New Viewpoints for *The New York Times,* pp. 295-302.

Rubinowitz, L. S. (1974), *Low-Income Housing: Suburban Strategies.* Cambridge, Mass.: Ballinger Publishing Company.

Sargent, C. S. (1974), "Rapid Transit and Urban Geography—A Primer for Phoenix," *High Speed Ground Transportation Journal,* 8:283-290.

*Schaeffer, K. H. and E. Sclar (1975), *Access for All: Transportation and Urban Growth.* Baltimore: Penguin Books, Inc.

Schiltz, T. and W. Moffitt (1971), "Inner City/Outer City Relationship in Metropolitan Areas: A Bibliographic Essay," *Urban Affairs Quarterly,* 7:75-108.

Schmitt, P. J. (1969), *Back to Nature: The Arcadian Myth in Urban America.* New York: Oxford University Press.

Schnall, Rabbi D. J. (1975), *Ethnicity and Suburban Local Politics.* New York: Praeger Publishers.

Schnore, L. F. (1972), *Class and Race in Cities and Suburbs.* Chicago: Markham Publishing Company (distributed by Rand McNally).

Schnore, L. F. and V. Z. Klaff (1972), "Suburbanization in the Sixties: A Preliminary Analysis," *Land Economics,* 48:23-33.

Schnore, L. F., C. D. André, and H. Sharp (1976), "Black Suburbanization, 1930-1970," in B. Schwartz (ed.), *The Changing Face of the Suburbs.* Chicago: The University of Chicago Press, pp. 69-94.

Schwartz, B. (1976a), "Images of Suburbia: Some Revisionist Commentary and Conclusions," in B. Schwartz (ed.), *The Changing Face of the Suburbs.* Chicago: The University of Chicago Press, pp. 325-340.

*_____ (ed.) (1976b), *The Changing Face of the Suburbs.* Chicago: The University of Chicago Press.

Schwirian, K. P. (ed.) (1974), *Comparative Urban Structure: Studies in the Ecology of Cities.* Lexington, Mass.: D. C. Heath and Company.

Scott, D. W. (1975), "Metropolitan Transaction Patterns in Suburban Chicago: The Case of School District Collaboration," *Publius,* Winter, 5:97-120.

Scott, T. M. (1975), "Implications of Suburbanization for Metropolitan Political Organization," *Annals of the American Academy of Political and Social Science,* 422:36-44.

Siembieda, W. J. (1975), "Suburbanization of Ethnics of Color," *Annals of The American Academy of Political and Social Science,* 422:118-128.

Singleton, G. H. (1973), "The Genesis of Suburbia: A Complex of Historical Trends," in L. H. Masotti and J. K. Hadden (eds.), *The Urbanization of the Suburbs.* Beverly Hills: Sage Publications, Urban Affairs Annual Reviews, 7:29-50.

Sobin, D. P. (1968), *Dynamics of Community Change: The Case of Long Island's Declining "Gold Coast".* Port Washington, N.Y.: Ira J. Friedman, Inc.

*_____ (1971), *The Future of the American Suburbs: Survival or Extinction?* Port Washington, N.Y.: Kennikat Press.

Sommer, J. W. (1975), "Fat City and Hedonopolis: The American Urban Future?" in R. Abler, D. Janelle, A. Philbrick, and J. Sommer (eds.), *Human Geography in a Shrinking World.* North Scituate, Mass.: Duxbury Press, pp. 132-148.

Stein, M. M. (1973), "Transportation and Metropolitan Growth: A Case Study of the Impact of Circumferential Highways on Intraregional Population Shifts." Paper presented at the Western Regional Science Association Meeting.

Sterne, M. (1974), "Jobs Drop 41,000 in City in a Year, Gain of 35,000 in Suburbs Fails to Offset Loss," *The New York Times,* August 17.

_____ (1975), "More Companies Here Seek Connecticut Sites," *The New York Times,* November 25, 1, 52.

_____ (1976), "Union Carbide, 3,500 on Staff, to Quit City," *The New York Times,* March 20, 1, 31.

Sternlieb, G. (1971), "The City As Sandbox," *Public Interest,* 25:14-21.

_____ (1972), "Death of the American Dream House," *Society,* February, 39-42.

Sternlieb, G., R. Burchell, and L. Sagalyn (1971), *The Affluent Suburb: Housing Needs and Attitudes.* New Brunswick, N.J.: Transaction Books.

Sternlieb, G. and W. P. Beaton (1972), *The Zone of Emergence: A Case Study of an Older Suburb.* New Brunswick, N.J.: Transaction Books.

Sternlieb, G. and R. W. Lake (1975), "Aging Suburbs and Black Homeownership," *Annals of the American Academy of Political and Social Science,* 422:105-117.

Suburban Action Institute (1970), *Open or Closed Suburbs: Corporate Location and the Urban Crisis.* Tarrytown, N.Y.: Suburban Action Institute.

Suffolk County Planning Commission (1974), *Suffolk County Office Building Study.* Hauppaugue, N.Y.: The Suffolk County Planning Commission.

Suttles, G. D. (1972), *The Social Construction of Communities.* Chicago: The University of Chicago Press.

*_____ (1975), "Community Design: The Search for Participation in a Metropolitan Society," in A. H. Hawley and V. P. Rock (eds.), *Metropolitan America in Contemporary Perspective.* New York: Halsted Press, Division of John Wiley & Sons, and Sage Publications, Inc., pp. 235-297.

Swatridge, L. A. (1972), *Problems in the Bosnywash Megalopolis: Pollution, Transportation, Sprawl, Social Problems.* Toronto: McGraw-Hill Ryerson Ltd.

Taeuber, K. E. (1975), "Racial Segregation: The Persisting Dilemma," *Annals of the American Academy of Political and Social Science,* 422:87-96.

*Tarr, J. A. (1973), "From City to Suburb: The 'Moral' Influence of Transportation Technology," in A. B. Callow, Jr. (ed.), *American Urban History: An Interpretive Reader With Commentaries,* 2nd rev. ed. New York: Oxford University Press, pp. 202-212.

Taylor, G. R. (1915, 1970), *Satellite Cities: A Study of Industrial Suburbs.* New York: Arno Press and *The New York Times.*

*Thorns, D. C. (1972), *Suburbia.* London: MacGibbon and Kee, Ltd.

*Time (1971), "Suburbia: The New American Plurality," *Time,* March 15, 14-20.

Tobin, G. A. (1976), "Suburbanization and the Development of Motor Transportation: Transportation Technology and the Suburbanization Process," in B. Schwartz (ed.), *The Changing Face of the Suburbs.* Chicago: The University of Chicago Press, pp. 95-111.

Trillin, C. (1976), "U.S. Journal: Mount Laurel, N.J.—Some Thoughts on Where Lines are Drawn," *New Yorker,* February 2, 69-74.

Tuan, Y.-F. (1974), *Topophilia: A Study of Environmental Perception, Attitudes, and Values.* Englewood Cliffs, N.J.: Prentice-Hall, Inc.

Ullman, E. L. (1962), "The Nature of Cities Reconsidered," *Papers and Proceedings of the Regional Science Association,* 9:7-23.

U.S. Bureau of the Census (1974), *Our Cities and Suburbs,* "We, The Americans" Series No. 7. Washington, D.C.

U.S. Department of Labor (1969), *Changes in Urban America,* Bureau of Labor Statistics Report No. 353. Washington, D.C.

U.S. Council on Environmental Quality et al. (1974), *The Costs of Sprawl: Environmental and Economic Costs of Alternative Residential Development Patterns at the Urban Fringe,* 3 Vols. Washington, D.C.

U.S. News and World Report (1971), "Are Big Cities Worth Saving?—Interview with George S. Sternlieb," July 26, 42-46, 49.

*_____ (1972), "New Role of the Suburbs," August 7, 52-56.

_____ (1973), "How Shopping Malls are Changing Life in U.S.," June 18, 43-46.

_____ (1974), "Shopping Centers of the Future: Smaller, More Fun," September 30, 67-68.

_____ (1976), " 'We're on Our Way to a Racial Showdown'—Interview with Roy Wilkins, Executive Director, NAACP," February 2, 74-75.

Vance, J. E., Jr. (1962), "Emerging Patterns of Commercial Structure in American Cities," in K. Norborg (ed.), *Proceedings of the I.G.U. Symposium in Urban Geography, Lund 1960.* Lund, Sweden: Royal University of Lund, Studies in Geography, Series B, No. 24, pp. 485-518.

_____ (1964), *Geography and Urban Evolution in the San Francisco Bay Area.* Berkeley: University of California, Berkeley, Institute of Governmental Studies.

_____ (1972), "California and the Search for the Ideal," *Annals of the Association of American Geographers,* 62:185-210.

Voorhees, A. M. (1970), "Urban Growth Characteristics," in R. G. Putnam, F. J. Taylor, and P. G. Kettle (eds.), *A Geography of Urban Places.* Toronto: Methuen Publications, pp. 81-86.

Wallace, W. N. (1971, 1974), "The Suburbanization of Professional Sports," in L. H. Masotti and J. K. Hadden (eds.), *Suburbia in Transition.* New York: New Viewpoints for *The New York Times,* pp. 109-110.

Walter, B. and F. M. Wirt (1972), "Social and Political Dimensions of American Suburbs," in B. J. L. Berry and K. B. Smith (eds.), *City Classification Handbook: Methods and Applications.* New York: John Wiley & Sons, Inc., pp. 97-123.

Ward, D. (1964), "A Comparative Historical Geography of Streetcar Suburbs in Boston, Massachusetts and Leeds, England: 1850-1920," *Annals of the Association of American Geographers,* 54:477-489.

_____ (1971), *Cities and Immigrants: A Geography of Change in Nineteenth Century America.* New York: Oxford University Press.

Ward, J. D. and N. G. Paulhus, Jr. (1974), *Suburbanization and Its Implications for Urban Transportation Systems.* Washington, D.C.: U.S. Department of Transportation, Office of R. & D. Policy.

*Warner, S. B., Jr. (1962), *Streetcar Suburbs: The Process of Growth in Boston, 1870-1900.* Cambridge, Mass.: Harvard University and the MIT Press. (Also published in paperback, New York: Atheneum, 1974).

_____ (1972), *The Urban Wilderness: A History of the American City.* New York: Harper & Row, Publishers.

Wattenberg, B. J. (1974), *The Real America.* Garden City, N.Y.: Doubleday and Company.

Webber, M. M. (1963), "Order in Diversity: Community Without Propinquity," in L. Wingo (ed.), *Cities and Space.* Baltimore: Johns Hopkins University Press, pp. 23-54.

_____ (1968), "The Post-City Age," *Daedalus,* 97:1091-1110.

Weber, A. F. (1899), *The Growth of Cities in the Nineteenth Century: A Study in Statistics.* New York: The Macmillan Company.

Williams, O. P., H. Herman, C. S. Liebman, and T. R. Dye (1965), *Suburban Differences and Metropolitan Policies.* Philadelphia: University of Pennsylvania Press.

Willie, C. V. (1974, 1975), "Life Styles of Black Families: Variations by Social Class," in S. D. Feldman and G. W. Thielbar (eds.), *Life Styles: Diversity in American Society,* 2nd rev. ed. Boston: Little, Brown and Company, pp. 406-417.

*Wilson, W. H. (1974), *Coming of Age: Urban America, 1915-1945.* New York: John Wiley & Sons, Inc.

*Wirt, F. M., F. F. Rabinovitz, and D. R. Hensler (1972), *On the City's Rim: Politics and Policy in Suburbia.* Lexington, Mass.: D.C. Heath and Company.

*Wood, P. A. (1974), "Urban Manufacturing: A View from the Fringe" in J. H. Johnson (ed.), *Suburban Growth: Geographical Processes at the Edge of the Western City.* London: John Wiley & Sons, Ltd., pp. 129-154.

Woodruff, A. M. (1974), "Recycling Urban Land," in C. L. Harriss (ed.), *The Good Earth of America: Planning Our Land Use.* Englewood Cliffs, N. J.: Prentice-Hall, Inc., pp. 31-66.

Yeates, M. H. and B. J. Garner (1976), *The North American City,* 2nd rev. ed. New York: Harper & Row, Publishers.

Zelinsky, W. (1973), *The Cultural Geography of the United States.* Englewood Cliffs, N.J.: Prentice-Hall, Inc.

_____ (1975), "Personality and Self-Discovery: The Future Social Geography of the United States," in R. Abler, D. Janelle, A. Philbrick, and J. Sommer (eds.), *Human Geography in a Shrinking World.* North Scituate, Mass.: Duxbury Press, pp. 108-121.

Zimmer, B. G. (1975), "The Urban Centrifugal Drift," in A. H. Hawley and V. P. Rock (eds.), *Metropolitan America in Contemporary Perspective.* New York: Halsted Press, Division of John Wiley & Sons, and Sage Publications, Inc., pp. 23-91.

Zikmund, J. (1967), "A Comparison of Political Attitude and Activity Patterns in Central Cities and Suburbs," *Public Opinion Quarterly,* 31:71-75.

_____ (1971), "Do Suburbanites Use the Central City?," *Journal of the American Institute of Planners,* 37:192-195.

_____ (1975), "Sources of the Suburban Population: 1955-1960 and 1965-1970," *Publius,* Winter, 5:27-44.

Zschock, D. K. (ed.) (1969), *Economic Aspects of Suburban Growth: Studies of the Nassau-Suffolk Planning Region.* Stony Brook, N.Y.: SUNY at Stony Brook, Economic Research Bureau.